DECLARING INDEPENDENCE

These United Colonies are, and of right ought to be, free and independent states. . . . They are absolved from all allegiance to the British Crown, and that all political connection between them . . . is, and ought to be, totally dissolved.

~Richard Henry Lee,
in a speech to the Continental Congress on June 7, 1776

DECLARING INDEPENDENCE

LIFE DURING THE AMERICAN REVOLUTION

BRANDON MARIE MILLER

LERNER PUBLICATIONS COMPANY · MINNEAPOLIS

To Jolene and Justin Marie, and their college diplomas. We're proud of your hard work!

And for all the men and women who faced tough choices in 1775, I dedicate this book.

A Word about Language

English word usage, spelling, grammar, and punctuation have changed over the centuries. In quoted material, this book preserves original language and spellings, including the now outdated term *negro*.

Lerner Publications Company
A division of Lerner Publishing Group
241 First Avenue North
Minneapolis, MN 55401 U.S.A.

Website address: www.lernerbooks.com

Library of Congress Cataloging-in-Publication Data

Miller, Brandon Marie.
    Declaring independence : life during the American Revolution / by Brandon Marie Miller.
        p.   cm. — (People's history)
    Includes bibliographical references and index.
    ISBN: 0–8225–1275–0 (lib. bdg. : alk. paper)
    1. United States—History—Revolution, 1775–1783—Social aspects—Juvenile literature. 2. United States—Social conditions—To 1865—Juvenile literature. I. Title. II. Series.
E209.M548 2005
973.3—dc22   200401791

Manufactured in the United States of America
1 2 3 4 5 6 – JR – 10 09 08 07 06 05

CONTENTS

This is the Place to affix the STAMP.

Every where it is the universal voice of all people, that if the stamp act must take place we are absolute slaves.

—Thomas Hutchinson, lieutenant governor of Massachusetts, 1760s

"THE PEOPLE ARE RIPE FOR MISCHIEF"

King George III of Great Britain had run out of patience. In November 1774, the king responded to grim dispatches from his royal officials in the American colonies. He wrote to his prime minister, Lord Frederick North, that "the New England Governments are in a state of rebellion, blows [fighting] must decide whether they are to be subject to this country or independent." The American colonists, the king noted, "are ripe for mischief." George III would not allow "dangerous men" in the colonies and their raggedy mobs to dictate Great Britain's policy.

The next year, on August 23, 1775, the king, sitting upon a velvet chair in James's Palace, scanned the royal proclamation awaiting his signature and seal. It began:

> Whereas many of our subjects . . . of our Colonies in North America, misled by dangerous . . . men, and forgetting the allegiance which they owe to the power that has protected and supported them . . . have . . . proceeded to open . . . rebellion . . . traitorously preparing . . . war against us.

The king snatched up a quill pen, jabbed the sharpened tip into black ink, and scratched his name across the top of the royal document: "George R" (Rex, Latin for king). There was more to the document, and it took on a more menacing tone.

British colonists in America rebelled against King George III (right) in the 1760s and 1770s. The colonists were most upset with what they saw as unfair taxation. Colonists replaced the king's tax stamp with one of their own design (opposite). The skull and crossbones stamp sent a clear message to the king: death to your document tax.

THE THIRTEEN AMERICAN COLONIES

Lake Superior

Lake Huron

Lake Michigan

Lake Ontario

Lake Erie

QUEBEC

Saint Lawrence River

Lake Champlain

MAINE
(part of
Massachusetts
until 1820)

Halifax

NEW
HAMPSHIRE

NOVA
SCOTIA

• Fort Niagara

Saratoga
Albany
Mohawk Valley

Concord
Lexington
Bunker Hill/Breed's Hill
Worcester
Charlestown
Boston

NEW YORK

Esopus
White Plains
New York City
Wyoming Valley
Morristown

Hudson River

Hartford

MASSACHUSETTS

Newport

Long Island

Brooklyn
Heights
Staten Island

RHODE ISLAND

CONNECTICUT

OHIO RIVER
VALLEY FRONTIER

PENNSYLVANIA

Valley Forge
Lancaster

Trenton
Philadelphia

NEW JERSEY

DELAWARE

Ohio River

APPALACHIAN MOUNTAINS

Annapolis

MARYLAND

Chesapeake Bay

VIRGINIA

Williamsburg
Richmond

Yorktown
Norfolk

INDIAN
RESERVE

Edenton

NORTH CAROLINA

Kings
Mountain

*ATLANTIC
OCEAN*

**Proclamation
Line of 1763**

SOUTH
CAROLINA

Cape
Fear

GEORGIA

Charleston

↑
N

Savannah

Miles

0   50   100   150   200

0   100   200   300

Kilometers

FLORIDA

Gulf of Mexico

■ The 13 American Colonies

All our Officers, civil and military, are obliged . . . to suppress such rebellion, and to bring the traitors to justice. . . . And we do strictly . . . command . . . our obedient and loyal subjects, to . . . suppress such rebellion . . . which they shall know to be against us, our crown [king and government] and dignity.

The king dripped a blob of molten red wax onto the document and shoved the royal seal into the wax. "A Proclamation, By the King, For Suppressing Rebellion and Sedition" was now official.

"A PROFIT TO THE NATION"

More than a century earlier, some European countries such as England had begun establishing colonies in far-off lands to enrich themselves with cash, goods, power, and glory. The English Parliament in the mid-1600s passed laws called navigation acts to regulate trade with its colonies. The ongoing laws required English colonists to buy most goods through British merchants—goods often sold to them at inflated prices. The acts also forbid colonists from making any items, even hats and buttons, that competed with articles produced in Great Britain. (In 1707 England, Scotland, and Wales united, forming Great Britain.)

At the same time, Britain expected the North American colonists to ship their products—rice, tobacco, corn, and fish—only to Great Britain and other British colonies, such as the West Indies in the Caribbean. Then English merchants sold these American products in Europe and Asia for profits that went to the British merchants.

Colonists also provided other raw materials. Their lumber built British ships. American furs and deerskins became fashionable hats in England. Indigo, a blue dye, went to British and Irish fabric makers. Americans sold the raw materials to Britain, and then they had to buy the expensive finished products from the mother country.

Some Americans profited from breaking Parliament's laws and avoiding high British prices. They stuffed ships with cheaper goods from countries such as France and smuggled them into the colonies past the king's custom (trade and tax) officials.

Even with smuggling, Lord Shelburne, an English politician, reported to Parliament in 1762 that the colonies provided "a clear profit to the Nation." Great Britain profited, but colonial resentment rose against the trade laws that provided wealth only to Britain. The colonists had to follow Britain's harsh trading laws, but they had no vote or elected representative in Britain's government.

VICTORY BRINGS NEW TENSIONS

Troubles between Great Britain and her thirteen colonies in North America exploded in the years after the French and Indian War (1754–1763). This war began when France, Britain's long-standing European rival, started expanding south from French Canada to build forts in American territory claimed by Great Britain. Twenty-one-year-old George Washington led the Virginia militia (citizen army) that joined British regular troops fighting French soldiers and their Native American allies on the Ohio River Valley Frontier. The fighting escalated, merging into a larger European conflict known as the Seven Years' War (1756–1763).

British victory in 1763 left that nation staggering from the cost of fighting the war. As part of the peace treaty, France handed over Canada and French lands east of the Mississippi River to Great Britain. Managing all these new territories further strained British finances. Clashes between white colonists itching to move west beyond the Appalachian Mountains and the Native Americans already living there caused more conflict.

In 1763 Parliament decided that protecting and running the North American empire drained too much money from Great Britain. The American colonies were no longer helpless infants requiring the mother country's constant care. More than two million people called the thirteen American colonies home. Most lived on farms, but cities

In this political drawing from the mid-1700s, colonists work at many different jobs in the city of Boston. For the benefit of Great Britain, King George and the British Parliament controlled industry and trade in the American colonies and imposed taxes on the colonists.

and towns also dotted the landscape. The British government felt that the colonists should share the expenses of British protection.

In 1763 the British government issued a proclamation, forbidding colonists from venturing west of the Appalachian Mountains. Parliament also hoped to prevent skirmishes with the Native Americans living there. And, as the royal governor of Georgia noted, better to keep the colonists "where they could be useful to their Mother Country, instead of planting themselves in the Heart of America, out of reach of Government."

Armed with swords and muskets, British customs officials search the home of colonists for illegal goods and to collect taxes owed the king by law.

The government also tightly enforced the trade laws that outlawed smuggling. Customs officials needed only a general search warrant, called a writ of assistance, to search peoples' homes for illegal goods. In Britain officials needed to show a good reason before they were allowed to enter and search a citizen's home.

"A POWER TO TAX"

The legislative assemblies elected in each colony had the power to tax the colonists. But Parliament decided to raise money through tax laws passed in Great Britain. Americans would have to pay these new taxes. In February 1765, Parliament debated a new tax on all legal papers, licenses, and publications used in the colonies—the Stamp Act. All documents would carry a stamp that showed the tax had been paid. Jared Ingersoll, the Connecticut agent (a person with the authority to act on behalf of others) in London, reported that some members of Parliament stood up for the colonists. They argued that "unless the Americans are allowed to send members to Parliament" to represent them, no new taxes ought to be passed for the colonies. Others, Ingersoll continued, replied that "a power to tax is a necessary part of every supreme legislative authority, and that if they have not that power over America . . . then America is at once a kingdom of itself."

Many people in Great Britain regarded Americans as rough and uneducated, a bit beneath a real Britain and not worth representation in Parliament. They felt superior to the people in the colonies. Benjamin Franklin wrote to a friend in Scotland that every Englishman wriggled onto the throne alongside King George to talk about "our subjects in the Colonies." This irked the Americans, who believed they possessed the same British rights as citizens living in London.

The Stamp Act passed, and it set off a flood of angry responses from the thirteen American colonies. In the Virginia legislature, called the House of Burgesses, twenty-nine-year-old Patrick Henry condemned the Stamp Act and compared George III to some of history's assassinated tyrants. When his speech raised shouts of treason, Henry shot back: "If this be treason, make the most of it!"

Patrick Henry (standing, center) *enrages members of the House of Burgesses with his condemnation of the Stamp Act in 1765. Ten years later, Henry would inspire Patriots—American colonists who supported the antitax cause and independence—and members of the same house by demanding, "Give me liberty or give me death."*

In May 1765, the Virginia Resolves passed the House of Burgesses. These resolutions declared that only the elected burgesses of Virginia had the "right and power to lay taxes . . . upon the inhabitants of this colony."

Other colonies were equally outraged by the Stamp Act. In August angry citizens of Boston—numbering in the thousands—hung, beheaded, and burned in effigy (a figure representing) the local stamp distributor, Andrew Oliver. The throng trooped to Oliver's offices and "pulled [the offices] down to the Ground in five minutes." Days later, a mob marched to the home of Thomas Hutchinson, who had been appointed lieutenant governor and chief magistrate by the king. Wielding axes, the mob splintered doors and furniture into kindling wood. They hacked down walls and left the home a hollow shell. They tore out gardens, drank wine, stole money, and ran off

In August 1765, Boston colonists rioted against the king's stamp tax. In this illustration from 1766 depicting the event, the riotous mob chases British official Thomas Hutchinson (above, center) from his home while others ransack it. In fact, Hutchinson and his family escaped just before the rebellious Bostonians arrived.

with anything left of any value. Mobs in other cities attacked their local stamp distributors and burned the officials in effigy.

In October 1765, representatives of eleven colonies held a Stamp Act Congress in New York. The Congress sent King George a petition (formal written statement or request) pledging their "affection and duty," then complained about Parliament's actions. The stamp tax, they pointed out, was unjust. Britain already reaped rewards from trade with the colonies. And since colonists had to buy goods from Great Britain, "they eventually contribute very largely to...the crown." They demanded Parliament repeal the Stamp Act and allow the colonies "the full and free enjoyments of their rights and liberties."

THE VULGAR MOB

The violent uproar over the Stamp Act sent shivers through many Americans. Massachusetts lieutenant governor Thomas Hutchinson, wrote with unease: "The authority is in the populace, no law can be carried into execution against their mind." The Massachusetts assembly [elected government], he continued,

> consists of the rabble of the town of Boston.... When there is occasion to hang or burn effigies or pull down houses these are employed. This flame...has been spread throughout this and every other colony.... There is no reasoning with them.

The king, warned Hutchinson, had better clamp the rabble back in their place.

In British society, place was important. Fashion, manners, wealth, and occupation marked a person's rank in society. The king, clad in velvet, silk, and the finest linen, stood at the top of society. Wealthy merchants, lawyers, and landowning farmers (referred to as "men of quality") were the leaders in the colonies. Slaves, free blacks, sailors, servants, laborers, and teenage apprentices (tradesmen in training)—

the lower ranks, as they were called—merged into the rabble, or mob. These inflamed "lower ranks" spilling into the streets filled "men of quality" with dread.

Many shared the view of Peter Oliver, chief justice of Massachusetts, that the mob were "perfect Machines, wound up by any Hand." Governor Morris of New York feared "the . . . mobility [mob] grow dangerous . . . and how to keep them down is the question. . . . If the disputes with Great Britain continue . . . we shall be under the domination of a riotous mob."

Many people from the upper classes also opposed the Stamp Act. Merchants and lawyers believed taxation without representation trampled on the colonists' basic rights as British subjects. These so-called Whigs, who objected to the new taxes and duties (taxes on imported goods), didn't approve of mob violence. But they needed support from a broad base of citizens—even the lower classes—to pressure Great Britain. And so the mob, the people, ordinary citizens, played a leading role in the growing divisions with the mother country.

The colonists' response to the Stamp Act stunned Britains. American merchants delayed paying their British creditors. Families bought fewer British goods. No British tax collector dared show his face on an American street. In 1766 Parliament repealed the hated Stamp Act. William Pitt, a leading political figure in Britain, observed that Great Britain should retain supreme power over the colonies, "except [for] taking their money out of their pockets without their consent."

DON'T BUY BRITISH GOODS!

A year after the Stamp Act repeal, though, Parliament passed the Townshend Acts (1767), taxing paper, lead, tea, and glass. Britain also sent more customs officials to try to stop the smuggling that robbed Britain of trade and tax revenues. Again, Americans protested. John Dickinson, a Pennsylvania lawyer, published *Letters from a Farmer in Pennsylvania* in December 1767. It was unfair, he wrote, that Great

This British political cartoon from 1766 shows British leaders in a funeral procession on the death of the Stamp Act. The cartoon criticizes Parliament for giving in to the demands of American colonists.

Britain forced colonists to buy goods only from Britain and then made them pay high taxes on those goods, as well. Dickinson considered the Townshend duties a form of slavery.

Once again, many colonist protested bitterly. "The mob," reported Hutchinson, "increased to two or three thousand chiefly sturdy boys and negroes and broke windows of the Comptrollers [accountant's] house and then the [customs] Inspectors."

Peter Oliver compared mobs to sheep and believed a few men, such as Boston's Samuel Adams, sparked the ignorant mobs into action. Adams belonged to the Sons of Liberty, powerful political committees that sprang up throughout the colonies during the Stamp Act crisis. The Sons of Liberty encouraged the mobs and joined with them to intimidate British officials. The Boston sheriff couldn't control the mobs—many of his men had joined the Sons of Liberty. The Boston branch of the Sons of Liberty sent a list of their grievances to the governor.

In July 1768, some merchants in Boston and Charleston, South Carolina, agreed not to import British goods for a year, except necessities such as salt, coal, medicines, nails, and gunpowder. Even citizens who frowned on mob violence could agree to the boycott and pledge not to buy from merchants carrying British goods.

The idea spread. A political committee in Lancaster, Pennsylvania, published the names of those who imported British goods and those who bought them. Hissing crowds surrounded these shops and frightened customers away. Others smashed shop windows and harassed British officials. Colonial tradesmen and craftspeople jumped at the chance to sell their own goods without competition from British imports.

A LIST of the Names of *those* who AUDACIOUSLY continue to counteract the UNITED SENTIMENTS of the BODY of Merchants thro'out NORTH-AMERICA; by importing British Goods contrary to the Agreement.

John Bernard,
(In King-Street, almost opposite Vernon's Head.

James McMasters,
(On Treat's Wharf.

Patrick McMasters,
(Opposite the Sign of the Lamb.

John Mein,
(Opposite the White-Horse, and in King-Street.

Ame & Elizabeth Cummings,
(Opposite the Old Brick Meeting House, all of Boston.

And, Henry Barnes,
(Trader in the Town of Marlboro'.

HAVE, and do still continue to import Goods from London, contrary to the Agreement of the Merchants.—They have been requested to Store their Goods upon the same Terms as the rest of the Importers have done, but absolutely refuse, by conducting in this Manner.

IT must evidently appear that they have preferred their own little private Advantage to the Welfare of America: It is therefore highly proper that the Public should know who they are, that have at this critical Time, forbidly detached themselves from the public Interest; and as they will be deemed Enemies to their Country, by all who are well-wishers to it; so those who afford them their Countenance or give them their Custom, must expect to be considered in the same disagreeable Light.

Broadsides (posted notices) and newspaper articles (left) advertised the names of American merchants who sold boycotted British goods. The notices and articles scorned the merchants. They also often warned colonists they would face disgrace if they broke the boycott and bought goods from the offending merchants. (Note: In the writings of the 1700s, the letter "s" often looked much like the letter "f.")

People hoped the boycott agreements would hurt the bank accounts of British merchants, who lost a fortune because of the boycott. The merchants would then pressure Parliament into repealing the new tax laws. Again, American outrage paid off. In April 1770, the Townshend Act—except for the tax on tea—was repealed.

THE WILD FRONTIER

Colonists in eastern cities were not the only ones turning anger into action. Colonists on the frontier also decided the time was ripe to protest injustices and demand their rights as citizens. Crippling taxes set by the colonial governments in the East angered western settlers. They also had a growing sense they were ignored by the easterners. The five western counties in Pennsylvania wrote to complain to the governor that they had fewer representatives in the colony's assembly than eastern counties. This was "oppressive, unequal, and unjust," the county representatives said.

Backcountry people also voiced their right to have local judges at trials and the chance to face a jury of their fellow frontier citizens. Court cases were tried in the East, forcing westerners to travel several hundred miles, at a loss of time and money.

Poor people in the West, living in one-room cabins on small farms, wanted to pay their taxes in produce or goods instead of scarce cash. In 1766 New York farmers refused to pay rising rents and taxes and rioted against their wealthy eastern landlords. Nearly 1,700 men gathered near Albany and broke open the jails in defiance. Many in the West insisted wealthy landowners should lower land rents, provide longer land leases, and force fewer families off the land.

Westerners also felt eastern governments ignored frontier safety. Frontier families, who were settling on Native American lands, bore the brunt of their raids. As Native Americans fought to save their lands, white settlers appealed for more government protection and help against them. Families on the frontier, they cried, lived in "the most extream distress." They felt the colonial governments protected Native Americans, while ignoring the plight of white settlers.

Frontier settlers in North and South Carolina also complained that their governments in the East did nothing to stop roving "gangs of villains" plundering frontier farms. Local citizens, "regulators" of the law, took matters into their own hands.

"We are free men," and British subjects, they complained, yet they had no share in the rights and benefits of good government. Many felt treated, not as brothers by the easterners, "but as if we were a different species."

"THIS HORRID MASSACRE"

In late September 1768, a British fleet dropped anchor in Boston Harbor. Sent by the government to occupy and control the rabble of Boston, four thousand British troops rowed ashore. Most soldiers lived

British soldiers fire into a crowd of peaceful American colonists in Paul Revere's engraving of the March 1770 "Boston Massacre" (below). *Revere sensationalized (exaggerated) the facts of the event in this engraving to stir the colonists' sympathy and anger and to draw them to the antitax cause.*

in barracks, but many quartered, or lived, in people's homes. There was one soldier for every four citizens. Everywhere people looked, soldiers patrolled in their bright red uniforms armed with swords, bayonets, and guns. Tensions mounted.

On March 5, 1770, a crowd numbering close to four hundred gathered around a handful of soldiers stationed outside the Boston Customs House. The crowd hurled insults and taunts as well as rocks and hunks of ice. The soldiers swung their guns to hold the crowds back.

No one knows who cried "Fire!"—a soldier or a voice from the jeering crowd. The frightened soldiers fired. Amid smoke and chaos five colonists lay dead—or dying—including a rope worker, two sailors, and two young apprentices. "The people were immediately alarmed with the report of this horrid massacre," reported the *Boston Gazette.* "The bells were set a-ringing, and great numbers soon assembled at the place where this tragical scene had been acted."

Thousands of citizens poured into the streets for the victims' funeral processions. Paul Revere, a Boston silversmith and engraver, made an engraving of the event, which many called the Boston Massacre. Revere depicted the mob as a group of meek and innocent men and called the British soldiers "savage" murderers with "bloody hands." The engraving further inflamed Patriot anger.

The *Boston Gazette* blamed the tragedy on "quartering troops among citizens in a time of peace." The troops pretended to support law and order. "But in reality," claimed the paper, the troops meant "to enforce oppressive measures, to awe and control the legislature . . . to quell a spirit of liberty."

It is a duty we owe, not only to our near and dear relations . . . but to ourselves.

—*fifty-one women of Edenton, North Carolina, signers of a nonimportation agreement, 1774*

"THEY FEEL THEIR IMPORTANCE"

Parliament had not repealed the tax on imported tea with the rest of the Townshend taxes. By 1773 Americans of all classes had embraced a tea boycott. Boycott leaders especially wooed the support of women as the family homemakers. "Yes Ladies," William Tennent III wrote encouragingly. "You have it in your power more than all your committees and Congresses, to strike the stroke" for American liberties.

A woman wrote a poem, "Address'd to the Daughters of Liberty in America" with the lines:

*Stand firmly resolved and bid Grenville [British politician] to see
That rather than Freedom, we'll part with our Tea.*

Hundreds of women signed pledges—not a drop of tea would pass their lips.

"A TEA POT OF THE HARBOR OF BOSTON"

In late November 1773, several ships loaded with chests of tea from the British East India Company, the official British tea merchants, sailed into Boston Harbor. Boycott leaders called public meetings to discuss the situation. Lieutenant Governor Hutchinson described one gathering: "principally of the Lower ranks of the People & even Journeymen Tradesmen . . . were not excluded yet there were . . . Gentlemen of Good fortunes among them." The tea tax had angered colonists in all walks of life.

Green Dragon Tavern, Boston, Mass., in 1773.

Opposite: *This exaggerated British cartoon mocks colonial women signing a no-tea pledge by making them look foolish. One group of colonists opposed to the tea tax met at the Green Dragon Tavern in Boston* (above) *to discuss their plans to disrupt British tea imports.*

Disgusted with the king's tea tax, colonists disguised as Mohawks raided British tea ships in Boston Harbor on December 16, 1773, dumping their cargo overboard. The act became known as the Boston Tea Party.

"Committee men & Mob Men," wrote a British official, pressured colonial merchants to refuse to sell the tea. But boycott leaders stressed the best way to show King George the colonists would not buy his tea was to make sure the tea chests were never unloaded. The ships must turn around and carry the tea back to Great Britain. Tea ships in New York and Philadelphia had returned to Britain with their cargoes of tea. But the ships anchored at Boston's Griffin's Wharf refused to leave.

On the night of December 16, a large throng nearing two thousand citizens massed along the wharf. Perhaps two hundred men and boys, dressed and painted as Mohawks to avoid identification, climbed on board the gently rocking ships. The crowd watched in near silence while the men ripped open 342 chests of tea and dumped the fragrant cargo over the ship's sides into Boston Harbor. The men were careful to destroy no other property, and the town lay quiet the rest of the evening. As the tide rose, splintered wood bobbed upon the water while expensive tea lapped against the shore-line. "It is said," wrote Chief Justice Peter Oliver, "that some of the Inhabitants of Boston would not eat of Fish caught in their Harbor, because they had drank of the *East India Tea.*"

"INTOLLERABLE" ACTS

King George and Parliament were furious. They vowed to make an example for all the colonies to see and fear. In 1774 Parliament passed the Boston Port Act. This bill closed Boston Harbor until the lost tea was paid for. Parliament also declared that all Massachusetts officials, even judges and sheriffs, would be appointed by the royal governor and responsible only to the king, not to the elected state assembly.

The king sent a military man, General Thomas Gage, as his new royal governor. George III expected Gage to force order and obedience upon Boston. The governor banned town meetings, except by his permission, and canceled the fall elections for the state assembly.

GENTLEMEN,

BY the last advices from London we learn that an Act has been passed by the British Parliament for blocking up the Harbour of Boston, with a Fleet of Ships of War, and preventing the Entrance in, or Exportation of, all Sorts of Merchandize, on Penalty of Forfeiture of the Goods and the Vessels which carry them : And not only the Goods and Vessels are to be forfeited, but the very Wharfinger who shall assist in lading or discharging such Goods or Merchandize, shall forfeit treble their Value, at their highest Price, together with his Cattle, Horses, Carriages, Implements whatsoever, made Use of in lading or landing them.

And under these grievous and unheard of Impositions are we to remain till his Majesty in Council shall be certified by the Governor or Lieutenant Governor, that a *full Obedience* is yielded to the *Laws* of a British Parliament, and the Revenue duly collected ; and also that the East-India Company have received full Satisfaction for their Teas, and the Revenue Officers, and others for their Sufferings, by their Endeavours to fix the Tea Duty upon us. And even then, the whole Port of *Boston* with all its Wharves, Quays, &c. shall be under the absolute Controul of his Majesty, and no Article of Merchandize landed on or laded from any of them, but such as he shall licence, on the Penalty aforesaid.

In 1774 King George and Parliament asserted their power in response to the Boston Tea Party, forcefully closing Boston Harbor with the Boston Port Act. This broadside notifies Bostonians of the passage and enforcement of the act.

This British political cartoon shows Bostonians in a cage hanging from the liberty tree, which is surrounded by British cannons, soldiers, and warships. British sailors feed the prisoners in exchange for promises to obey the king and Parliament. The cartoon criticizes the colonists' rebellion and their useless attempts to resist Great Britain.

Those loyal to the king felt Boston had brought this wrath upon itself. "Their opposition to Good Government," wrote the Reverend William Clarke, "has . . . been shamefully flagrant. . . . His Majesty . . . resents it to the highest Degree." But many colonists labeled these measures the "Intollerable Acts."

Demonstrations against the Intolerable Acts broke out across the colonies. Committees of Correspondence, formed in each colony, wrote letters to spread the news from Boston to the other colonies. Sympathy and offers of assistance poured into Massachusetts. New York's committee sent concern for "a Sister Colony suffering in Defense of the Rights of America." But, they added, "what ought to be done . . . is very hard to determine."

The Connecticut Sons of Liberty burned a copy of the Intolerable Acts while one thousand people gathered around to watch. Virginia's House of Burgesses in Williamsburg set aside a June day for prayer on behalf of Boston. When Virginia's royal governor dissolved the official House of Burgesses, the legislators [lawmakers] met anyway, moving up the street from their meetinghouse to the Raleigh Tavern.

THE KING LOSES CONTROL

The Crown's newly declared control of who would serve as colonial judges, sheriffs, marshals, and justices of the peace outraged Massachusetts citizens. The people's elected representatives had always approved these positions. People feared they would be unable to throw out a corrupt judge or sheriff. Corrupt officers could gain power over their neighbors, and the people were powerless to have them removed from office. Citizens again sprang into action.

In September, when the judges appointed by the king arrived in Worcester, Massachusetts, they faced a throng of five thousand to six thousand determined people. The crowd formed into two lines, and the judges, sheriffs, and lawyers passed between them, their hats clutched in their hands as a sign of respect. The crowd forced the men to declare they wouldn't hold court (official legal sessions) under the new acts of Parliament. Then they forced them to resign.

The king and his officials lost control in many parts of Massachusetts. Lieutenant Governor Thomas Oliver resigned when four thousand people surrounded his house. "In compliance with their commands, I sign my name [to the resignation]," he wrote. Royal officials in other parts of Massachusetts raced to Boston, seeking the protection of British troops. Even General Gage admitted this rejection of royal appointees was the work, not of a rabble, "but the Freeholders and Farmers of the Country." Working through committees and associations, citizens took over many of the roles the king had stripped from the local government.

Printed in 1782, this engraving by François Godefroy shows the First Continental Congress in session at Carpenters' Hall in Philadelphia, Pennsylvania, during September 1774. Representatives of twelve colonies met to discuss what should be done about the mounting dispute with Great Britain.

FIRST CONTINENTAL CONGRESS

Each colony wondered if it would be the next to feel Britain's wrath. All colonies but Georgia agreed to send representatives to a Continental Congress—a formal meeting in Philadelphia. Delegates would decide how to deal with the Intolerable Acts and the troubles in Massachusetts.

In October, William Eddis of Maryland wrote, "The general attention is fixed on the Congress now sitting in Philadelphia, and all descriptions of people are waiting for the result of their deliberations with the utmost impatience." Eddis hoped the Congress and the king would peacefully settle "these growing differences. The colonies are daily gaining incredible strength," he added. "They *know,* they *feel,* their importance; and *persuasion,* not *force,* must retain them in obedience."

On October 1, 1774, the Congress sent the king a Declaration of Colonial Rights and Grievances. British liberty, they argued, included the right of representation in the legislatures. British liberty included the right to gather, voice complaints, and petition the king. The Continental Congress also asked Parliament to repeal acts calling for taxes and duties. They wanted Boston Harbor opened. They argued that keeping an army in the colonies in times of peace, without the consent of their colonial legislatures, was against the law. "To these grievous acts and measures, Americans cannot submit."

A few days later, the Congress passed the Continental Association—a nonimportation agreement. For one year, colonists would not import or buy goods from Great Britain. They hoped this boycott of British goods would hit British merchants, who would then pressure Parliament to lift the duties. Congress adjourned (ended) but agreed to meet again in the spring if the situation had not improved.

In towns throughout the colonies, local committees tracked who did and did not uphold the nonimportation agreement. One committee gave notice that "all such foes to the rights of British-America may be publickly known, and universally condemned as the enemies of American liberty; and thence forth we . . . will break off all dealing with him or her."

One Boston broadside singled out William Jackson, an importer. "It is desired that the SONS and DAUGHTERS of LIBERTY, would not buy any one thing of him, for in so doing they will bring Disgrace upon *themselves,* and their *Posterity* [children], for *ever* and *ever.*"

"A SPECTACLE OF HORROR"

Americans began labeling one another with great scorn. Those loyal to the king sneered at the antitax colonists, calling them rebels. With equal disgust, the rebels—who called themselves Patriots or Whigs—branded Loyalists as Tories after the ruling party in Britain.

Violence against those loyal to the king escalated from taunting and shaming to whippings, beatings, and tarring the victim. Anne Hulton, a Loyalist, described the tarring of one man. His arm was dislocated when the mob tore off his clothes. They then poured hot tar over his body.

He was drag'd in a Cart with thousands attending, some beating him w'th clubs & knocking him out of the Cart. . . . They gave him several severe whippings, at different parts of the Town. This Spectacle of horror and sportive cruelty was exhibited for about five hours. . . . The Doctors say that it is impossible this poor creature can live. They say his flesh comes off his back.

Loyalist minister Mather Byles believed it his duty to support the king, though he wished George III would mend his policies toward America. As he watched a mob of rebels gather in his town, Byles wrote a friend: "They call me a brainless Tory; but tell me, my young

Colonists prepare to tar and feather a British customs officer on a crowded street in the American colonies. Tarring and feathering can be deadly, in addition to being painful and humiliating. As tensions mounted between colonists and Great Britain, opposition grew increasingly violent.

friend, which is better—to be ruled by one tyrant three thousand miles away, or by three thousand tyrants not a mile away?"

The violence plunged the British government in America into chaos. "There's no Magistrate [judge] that dare . . . act to suppress the outrages," Anne Hulton wrote. Virginia royal governor Lord Dunmore complained, "There is not a Justice of the Peace in Virginia that acts, except as a committee man." For those who supported the Crown, the future appeared bleak and "must inevitably be dreadful," noted William Eddis.

"THE ENTHUSIASM OF THE SPINNING WHEEL"

Women were not supposed to ruffle their brains with politics. Politics belonged to men, whose minds were considered stronger. But the large-scale boycott of British goods touched the lives of most women. They had to work even harder making items they could no longer buy.

Without women's support, the boycott would fail. Christopher Gadsten wrote an open letter to citizens of South Carolina and urged husbands to convince their wives "that it is the only thing that can save them and their children, from distresses, slavery, and disgrace."

Women organized spinning bees to make cloth. Wearing homespun gowns instead of imported British fabrics became a badge of patriotism. Clergymen who supported the boycott "preached about it & about it, untill the Women and Children . . . set their Spinning Wheels a whirling in Defiance of Great Britain," wrote Peter Oliver in disgust.

Many females quite liked the taste of talking politics. How could women remain silent "when the subject is so very interesting . . . & what every Member of the Community is more or less concerned in?" asked Anne Emlen. Upper-class women—"Ladies of the highest rank and influence"—carried out much of the patriotic efforts. With houses filled with fine furniture and delicate china, among other imported luxuries, they had the most to sacrifice for the cause.

TO FREE THEMSELVES FROM SLAVERY

Those who enjoyed the least luxuries were the 500,000 African Americans who lived in the thirteen colonies. Most were slaves. They listened intently to the political talk around them as white Americans accused Britain of enslaving the colonies and stealing their political freedoms.

So while white citizens battled the tea tax and petitioned the king and Parliament, four African American men petitioned their local assemblyman.

> *Sir, The efforts made by the legislature of this province . . . to free themselves from slavery, gave us, who are in that deplorable state, a high degree of satisfaction. We expect great things from men who have such a noble stand against the designs of their fellow-men to enslave them.*

Most white Americans spoke about protecting their rights as British subjects. But African Americans saw a larger issue. Didn't all people have a natural right to freedom? In May 1774, a small group of blacks appealed to the Massachusetts's governor and council.

> *We have in common with all other men a natural right to our freedoms with out Being depriv'd of them by our fellow men as we are a freeborn Pepal . . . Brought hither to be made slaves for Life.*

African Americans wondered how the troubles between Great Britain and the colonies would affect them. Some blacks joined the protesting mobs. Crispus Attucks, a former slave, was killed in the Boston Massacre. Other enslaved African Americans wondered if their best chance for freedom lay with the British.

Abigail Adams was the wife of Boston lawyer John Adams, who served in the Continental Congress. In June 1774, Abigail wrote John

Laſt Thurſday, agreeable to a general Requeſt of the Inhabitants, and by the Conſent of Parents and Friends, were carried to their *Grave* in Succeſſion, the Bodies of *Samuel Gray, Samuel Maverick, James Caldwell,* and *Criſpus Attucks,* the unhappy Victims who fell in the bloody Maſſacre of the Monday Evening preceeding !

This 1770 Boston newspaper article reports the deaths of four of the colonists killed during the Boston Massacre, including Crispus Attucks (inset). Attucks, a former slave, was a sailor living in the Boston area.

about reported rumors that Massachusetts slaves planned to petition the royal governor with an offer to fight for him in exchange for freedom.

Liberty, freedom, obedience, and rights—the words tugged on people's thoughts, blacks as well as whites. In 1775 Joshua Eden placed an advertisement in the *South Carolina Gazette* for his runaway slave, Limus. Anyone finding Limus could whip him, "for though he is my Property, he has the audacity to tell me, he will be free, that he will serve no Man, and that he will be conquered or governed by no Man." Many slaves, like Limus, claimed the cause of liberty and freedom as their own.

While we . . . love our mother country, her sword is opening our veins.
—John Dickinson, April 19, 1775

"YOU ARE NOW MY ENEMY"

By 1775 there were nearly 6,500 British soldiers occupying Boston. They made sure that no trade ships entered the harbor. They controlled entrance to the city, which connected to the rest of the colony by a narrow strip of land, called Boston Neck. With the harbor closed, businesses had nothing to sell and people's jobs vanished. Food grew scarce. Some families survived by eating rats. Other families bought food smuggled into the city at night from surrounding farms and villages. With few supplies coming into town, people were forced to tear down fences, ship wharves, buildings, even church pews for firewood.

In the towns outside Boston, volunteers organized into militias and drilled regularly on village greens in case they were needed to protect their homes from British soldiers. General Gage reported to the king that the rebels collected weapons and ammunition to supply, "a Body of Troops to act in opposition to His Majesty's Government." They'd hidden the arms in the town of Concord. In the spring of 1775, Gage ordered seven hundred soldiers to seize the stockpiled ammunition and weapons.

"DISPERSE, YE REBELS!"

Patriot leaders in Boston learned of Gage's plan. During the night of April 18, Paul Revere and others galloped out of the city to warn people in the countryside: the British are coming!

British soldiers ferried across Boston's Charles River and marched to Lexington, closing in on the weapon stash at Concord. As the sun rose, touching orchards white with apple blossoms, the British spied shadowy figures dashing through fields. Militia men from scattered farms raced to face the British troops.

Opposite: British soldiers and colonial militia clash during the Battle of Lexington in 1775. Paul Revere as painted by John S. Copley in 1768 (right). *Prior to the battle, Revere and two other men set out from Boston for Lexington and Concord on April 18, 1775. The men were to warn militia of the approaching British army. The British captured Revere. One rider turned back to Boston. The other made it to Concord.*

"Disperse, ye rebels!" cried the British commander Major John Pitcairn. It was clear to all that the British outnumbered the eighty men in the militia. Pitcairn ordered his men not to fire. But in those anxious moments, with their heart's drumming against their chests and fingers tensed on the triggers, someone—British or American—did fire. That single shot unleashed a British volley that shrouded the road with smoke and noise. British officers shouted, waving their swords, struggling to keep their men under control. Eight Americans lay dead, and nine others were wounded. The rest of the militia scattered for cover. With only one British soldier injured, the redcoats (a nickname for British troops, who wore red jackets) continued their advance toward Concord.

About 150 militia men awaited the British in Concord. The *Pennsylvania Journal* later reported that "the troops of Britain's King" fired first at "his loyal American subjects, and put a period [an end] to ten lives before one gun was fired upon them!" Hidden behind stone fences, houses, and woodpiles, the Americans returned fire. Church bells clanged the alarm, and word raced through the countryside nearly as fast as the bullets whizzing through the air.

Men from other towns galloped to support Concord. As the day wore on, eventually more than three thousand colonists came together to fight the British. "These fellows were generally good marksman," wrote Frederick MacKenzie, a British officer.

As the Americans closed in, the British retreated—even when two thousand more British soldiers met them on the road. With the Americans dogging every step, they fought through towns and villages all the way back to Charlestown, just across the river from Boston. Gage reported 73 men killed and 174 wounded.

The Americans lost 49 men, and another 48 colonists were wounded at Concord. But on that long day, April 19, 1775, townsmen, farmers, youthful apprentices, businessmen, and African Americans had stood against one of the finest equipped and best-trained armies in the world. Peter Oliver wrote, "After the Battle of Lexington, there was a general Uproar through the Neighboring Colonies. . . .

Colonial militia from Concord engage British troops at Concord Bridge on April 19, 1775. Though greatly outnumbered, the local militia, joined by others from nearby towns, managed to block the British advance.

In the Spring of 1775," Oliver added, "the War began to redden [turn bloody]."

"MY UNHAPPY COUNTRY"

People waged a war of words on street corners and over tavern tables. Ministers lectured from church pulpits. Fear, confusion, and outrage splashed across newspapers and in private letters.

John Dickinson sadly wrote his friend Arthur Lee that the "war of tyranny against innocence, has commenced [begun] in the neighborhood of Boston." Yet Dickinson, like most Americans, hoped the colonies and Great Britain could reconcile. Still loyal to the king, Dickinson didn't want to see the relationship between the colonies and Britain destroyed by war. He hoped the British government would see how its actions had driven Americans to unite against the mother country.

"May that God . . . speedily restore peace and liberty to my unhappy country," wrote Isaac Wilkins. "May Great Britain and America be soon united . . . a happy Nation to the end of time." Others feared Great Britain's actions would force war. Benjamin Franklin wrote a British friend, William Strahan, in July:

> *You are a Member of Parliament, and one of the Majority which has doomed my Country to Destruction. You have begun to burn our Towns, and murder our People. Look upon your Hands! They are stained with the Blood of your Relations! You and I were long Friends: You are now my Enemy, and I am Yours.*

The coming conflict also tore apart the relationship between Franklin and his son. William Franklin was a Loyalist and the royally appointed governor of New Jersey.

A South Carolina minister left members of his church in tears as he preached of "entering into a dreadful civil war; the worst of wars! And, what was most to be lamented, it could not be avoided."

A French artist created this painting of Benjamin Franklin in the 1770s. Franklin was like many colonists who faced making difficult decisions on the issue of independence. Franklin broke his long relationships with British friends and even with his Loyalist son, uncertain if the bonds could ever be restored.

Loyalists at a gathering in White Plains, New York, signed a paper denouncing congresses and committees that bullied their neighbors. "We are determined at the hazard of our lives and properties to support the king and [British] constitution." Frontiersmen in Anson County in North Carolina wrote their royal governor they were proud members of, "the glory of the British Empire and the envy of all Nations around it." Many viewpoints, much confusion, and much anger were sweeping through the American colonies.

"HOW DISMAL WAS THE SIGHT"

On April 22, 1775, Gage reported that several thousand New England militia men circled Boston "threatening an Attack, and getting up Artillery [cannon]. And we are very busy in making Preparations to oppose them." Eighteen days later, on May 10, a second Continental Congress gathered in Philadelphia to discuss the dangerous and disintegrating situation.

On the night of June 16, New England militias used the cover of darkness to fortify Breed's Hill and Bunker Hill. These hills overlooked Charlestown and the Charles River to British-occupied Boston beyond. In the early hours of dawn on June 17, British naval officers discovered the American troops dug into the hills. Warships began blasting Breed's Hill. Cannon roar echoed over land and water. That afternoon two thousand British troops crammed onto barges and ferried from Boston across the Charles River. Once landed, they formed into long, crimson rows and stormed up the slope.

The Americans held their ground, waiting until they stared into the faces of British soldiers only fifteen feet away—then they fired. Wave after wave of redcoats fought up the hillsides in the blazing sun. Eventually, the Americans ran out of ammunition and had to retreat.

More than one thousand men lay dead on the trampled, bloody hillside. Below, Charlestown burned. "How Dismal was the Sight," Boston citizen Samuel Webb wrote his brother, "to see the Beautiful

Published in 1783, this engraving shows the 1775 British assault on Charlestown, Massachusetts, and the Battle of Bunker Hill (right center).

& Valuable town of Charlestown all in Flames—and now behold it a heap of Ruins—with nothing Standing but a heap of chimneys." People had once lived in those homes. They were the first of thousands of Americans uprooted by the war.

In Connecticut, Joseph Fish's family heard news that a young relative had been killed at Breed's Hill. "We mourned for him with bitterness," remembered Joseph, until news arrived a week later that the lad was alive and well. In an era without instant communications, rumors spread like wildfire and many families waited months to hear the fate of loved ones or never heard at all.

"NO RANTING SWEARING FELLOW"

Just days before New Englanders fought the king's troops at Breed's Hill, the Continental Congress decided on June 14 to form a Continental army to defend the country. The New England militias around Boston became the base of this new army, and other colonies would send men to swell the ranks. Congress authorized enlisting up to twenty thousand men. They also voted to create a "Continental Currency, and have ordered two Million Dollars to be Struck for payment of the troops," George Washington reported to his brother-in-law. The Continental Congress had to take out loans to cover expenses, for they had no power to raise money by taxing the colonies.

Congress voted unanimously to offer the job of leading the army to forty-three-year-old Washington, a Virginian. On June 17, John Adams, still a Massachusetts member of Congress, wrote to his wife Abigail that American liberties depended to a great degree upon Washington. That same day, Eliphalet Dyer, a Connecticut member of Congress, wrote a friend his observations of Washington. The Virginian, he felt, would get along well with New England soldiers. "He is a Gentleman, highly Esteemed by those acquainted with him," wrote Dyer. "He is Clever, & if any thing too modest He seems discre[e]t & Virtuous, no harum Starum [wild] ranting Swearing fellow but Sober, steady, & calm."

Washington took command of the army at Cambridge, Massachusetts, on July 3, 1775. Most congressmen feared that a long-term, large army might grow too loyal to a leader like Washington. They decided to make the soldier enlistment period last only until the end of 1775. Local militias already served for only a short time.

"THE MOST FRUGAL MANNER POSSIBLE"

On July 16, 1775, Abigail Adams wrote to her husband in Philadelphia from their farm outside Boston. She scolded John for sending her hastily scrawled letters, some with only six lines.

For his part, John hungered for news of Boston and the countryside. Abigail warned him that her information was shaped by rumors, but she reported all beef was gone, malt and cider—gone.

The upheavals in Boston made trade difficult, and most supplies went to the British soldiers. Nor could people buy rum, for every drop went to the redcoats. Fresh foods were saved for the sick and wounded. Curfews cleared the streets after ten o'clock at night, unless you carried a pass from General Gage. Trade goods, such as pepper, from the South Pacific islands, were nearly impossible to find. She missed "common small articles which are not manufactured amongst ourselves. . . . Not one pin is to be purchased for love nor money." Abigail and their four children lived "in the most frugal manner possible, but I am many times distressed. Do let me know if there is any prospect of seeing you?" she begged. "Next Wednesday is thirteen weeks since you went away."

Smallpox and the intestinal disease dysentery also invaded New England. They spread through crowded army camps. And as soldiers marched, or militiamen returned home, they carried disease to the people. Abigail Adams took the then unusual step of inoculating (vaccinating) her family against smallpox. She hoped that by having a pox virus scratched into her children's skin, they would develop a resistance to the killer disease and be safe from future infections. But the inoculation carried risks. Sometimes people died from the inoculation virus or passed the disease onto others.

AN OLIVE BRANCH

On July 5, 1775, the Congress approved the humble Olive Branch Petition proposed by John Dickinson. This petition, a gesture of goodwill, proclaimed the colonies' devotion to the king and mother country. In the petition, the Congress blamed government ministers for forcing colonists "to arm in our own defense, and have engaged us in a controversy." The petition said that most Americans desired "the former harmony" between Great Britain and the colonies restored. It asked the king to use his "royal authority and influence" and grant the colonies relief.

But when the Olive Branch Petition reached London, George III refused to even read it. He answered, on August 23, 1775, by signing the royal proclamation declaring his American subjects to be in a state of rebellion.

Matters did not improve as 1775 wore on. General William Howe replaced Gage as commander in chief of the British armies. American troops marched toward Canada hoping to deprive British soldiers of a base in the north. But in December, the British defeated the colonial army at Quebec.

Meanwhile, Washington and other American soldiers surrounded Boston. That fall Martha Washington had joined her husband in neighboring Cambridge. In December she wrote a friend, "Some days we have a number of cannon and shells from Boston and Bunkers Hill, but it does not seem to surprise any one but me; I confess I shudder every time I hear the sound of a gun." Having never before seen anything of war, "the preparations, are very terable indeed," she confided.

"YOU INDIANS ARE NOT CONCERNED"

As American and British soldiers fought each other in the East, agents for both sides rushed to meet with Native Americans on the frontier. In July 1775, an American delegation met in Albany, New York, with members of the Iroquois League: Mohawks, Onondagas, Oneidas, Senecas, Cayugas, and Tuscaroras. The British had a long-term friendship with these native peoples. The American delegation hoped to persuade the Native Americans to remain neutral.

The American agents explained how the British "slip their hand into our pocket without asking" and take money, according to a message from the Continental Congress. They said the king's ministers shut the royal ears "to the cries of his children in America." Most important, the agents said, "This is a family quarrel between us and Old England. You Indians are not concerned in it. . . . We desire you to remain at home, and not join either side." If the British treated the

Mohawk leaders such as Tiyanoka (shown at right in a British uniform) had established alliances with the British military during the French and Indian Wars. British agents hoped these relationships would remain in place during the war against the American colonists. They were disappointed.

Americans this way, they added, "who are the same blood as themselves, what can you, who are Indians, expect from them afterwards?"

The British, however, hoped to keep the Native Americans as war allies. John Butler, the British agent, reminded the tribes that "your Father the Great King has taken pity on you." The Americans, warned Butler, would cheat the Iroquois, "take all your Lands from you and destroy your people for they are all mad, foolish, crazy and full of deceit."

But the Native American response at this point was less than Butler hoped. Mohawk chief Little Abraham answered that his people would gladly "sit still and see you fight it out." And Kayashute, a Seneca chief, scornfully replied that his people could defend themselves without British help.

LORD DUNMORE'S PROCLAMATION

As British authority crumbled in towns and villages, many of the royal governors fled, including Lord Dunmore, governor of Virginia. He abandoned the capital of Williamsburg for a British warship in the Chesapeake Bay. Before he fled, Dunmore issued a proclamation in November 1775 that sent shock waves through the colonies. He promised freedom to Virginia servants and slaves who ran away from rebel masters and joined his majesty's troops.

Slave owners lived in fear of a bloody slave revolt. The British, declared one slave owner from Maryland, encouraged the slaves "to cut their masters' throats while they sleep." Others complained that Dunmore's Proclamation was an excuse to steal slaves who were the property of Patriots, while Dunmore and other Loyalists kept their own slaves. A letter published in the *Virginia Gazette* on November 24, 1775, pointed out that Dunmore had no use for "the aged, the infirm, the women and children, [who] are still to remain the property of their masters." The slaves left behind would surely be watched carefully by their owners and face harsh punishments for the slightest defiance.

But thousands of Virginia's enslaved saw the contest between Britain and her colonies as a ticket to freedom they could not ignore. Slaves had always run away. The proclamation gave them a clear destination—wherever the king's army camped. Virginian Landon Carter dashed off a diary entry for June 26, 1776. Nine of his male slaves had stolen clothes and guns and run away during the night, "run away, to be sure, to Lord Dunmore."

A month after his proclamation, Dunmore had enlisted nearly two thousand black men to serve in his regiment. But when Dunmore's ships departed the Virginia coast eight months later, in June 1776, only about three hundred of those African Americans were still alive. Most were killed by disease that spread through the British ships housing the refugees. If not for the sickness, Dunmore claimed, "I should have had two thousand blacks; with whom I should have had no doubt of penetrating into the heart of this colony."

Yet through all the Gloom I can see Rays of ravishing Light and Glory.
—*John Adams, July 3, 1776*

"FREE AND INDEPENDENT STATES"

In January 1776, Thomas Paine, an Englishman who'd moved to America only a year earlier, published a forty-seven-page pamphlet called *Common Sense*. Carefully and logically written in words the average person could understand, Paine outlined a new idea—the reasons the colonies ought to break off from Great Britain. Within months, more than 100,000 copies of *Common Sense* had flown off the printing presses—nothing before had ever sold so well. In newspapers, in town meetings, in assemblies and committees, in taverns and across the dinner table, Americans discussed Paine's pamphlet.

Paine blamed not only Parliament and British government ministers for the current hostilities. He also lay blame at the feet of King George III. "A thirst for absolute power is the natural disease of monarchy," claimed Paine.

Paine took every argument for remaining under Great Britain's wing and turned it upside down. The colonies, he argued, would fare better without Britain's clutching hands. "Our corn will fetch its price in any market in Europe," Paine reminded people, "and our imported goods must be paid for, buy them where we will."

Britain "did not protect us from our enemies on our account," read *Common Sense,* "but from her enemies on her own account." America had only tasted war because Britain dragged the colonies into European conflicts.

Paine asserted Great Britain could not truly even be called the mother country of the colonies, because people from all over Europe had immigrated to the American colonies.

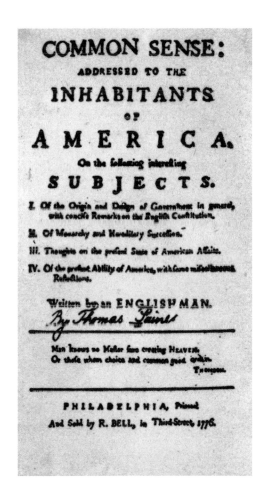

Opposite: *The colonial army's first decisive military victory at Boston in 1776. The title page to Thomas Paine's* Common Sense (right). *Published in 1776,* Common Sense *outlined Paine's persuasive argument for independence from Great Britain. More than 100,000 copies of the book sold within the first few months of publication.*

"This new World [America] hath been the asylum for . . . lovers of . . . liberty from every part of Europe," he noted.

Then Thomas Paine championed the cause of independence. Only independence, he said, could ensure peace in America. And in place of a king, Paine hoped Americans could boast, "THE LAW IS KING."

"O ye that love mankind! Ye that dare oppose not only the tyranny, but the tyrant, stand forth!" Let all Americans become "supporter[s] of the RIGHTS OF MANKIND, and of the FREE AND INDEPENDENT STATES OF AMERICA."

Many Americans hadn't been sure what they believed about the conflict between Britain and the colonies. Others opposed British policies but were not prepared to embrace a radical, unachievable idea like independence. Now, however, Paine's words inspired, formed, and sharpened the beliefs of thousands of Americans. Independence no longer loomed as an unthinkable goal.

Events in Europe also propelled some undecided colonists toward independence. That January, George III's October speech to Parliament arrived in America. The king blasted the American rebels and announced he would hire Hessian (German) troops to help smother the rebellion.

This 1776 British political cartoon shows King George III watching (window, at left) as Parliament forges shackles for the American colonies. The cartoon illustrates the punishing response of British leadership to the American colonists' talk of rebellion.

The idea that their own king would send foreign troops to slaughter them horrified even loyal colonists.

From across the sea came whispers that France and Spain, Britain's old enemies, welcomed trouble between Britain and its colonies. If colonists could persuade powerful France and Spain to aid the American cause, then independence—which would surely mean war— could actually be achieved.

LOYALIST CHOICES

Other Americans felt that Parliament may indeed have gone too far, while independence still remained unimaginable. They stayed proudly loyal to the king, Parliament, and the most powerful nation on earth.

Peter Van Schaack, a wealthy New Yorker, felt events had moved too quickly from questioning how much "subordination [obedience] we owe to the British Parliament" to "whether we are members of the empire or not." Van Schaack did not believe Parliament passed laws with a "plan of enslaving us. . . . Some kind of dependence," he confided to his journal, was "necessary for our happiness."

Over the winter, Washington's troops circled Boston, some positioned within a thousand yards of the town. These soldiers were able to cut off supplies to the British entering Boston by land. By the end of March, with their food rations dwindling, the British decided to evacuate (leave) the city. Howe sent word to Washington that the Americans must let the British leave without trouble, otherwise he would burn Boston to the ground.

News of the evacuation spread quickly. Most citizens rejoiced, but shocked Loyalists panicked. They couldn't imagine life without the protection of the mother country. Dr. Sylvester Gardiner, a Loyalist, knew he couldn't stay in Boston "and trust my person with a set of lawless rebels whose actions have disgraced human nature and who have great cruelty." Loyalists had only days to make their decision, gather money, and pack their belongings. In the end, most who fled

This engraving from 1776 shows the British evacuating Boston in March of that year. Following a successful siege of Boston by Washington and the colonial army, hungry and undersupplied British forces had little choice but to leave.

left almost everything behind. Some found they could not go at all—the departing British ships had no more room.

Nearly 20,000 people crammed on board the British ships: soldiers, king-appointed officials and their families, and more than 1,100 Loyalists. In the crush of bodies, one man reported, "a great many Children was Sufficated the first night."

The refugees landed at Halifax, Nova Scotia (in Canada). With the large number of arrivals flooding the city, costs for food and firewood soared. Dr. Gardiner cursed the rebellion that drove him to "this miserable place" and reduced him to poverty. "God only knows what I shall do," he wrote.

Many refugees eventually made their way to Great Britain, still homesick for America. They crowded into the cities, looking for work, a government post, a place in society. The former Massachusetts lieutenant governor Thomas Hutchinson penned in his diary,

"Some of us at first coming, are apt to think ourselves of importance, but other people do not think so."

TENSE DAYS IN PHILADELPHIA

In Philadelphia the Continental Congress continued to discuss how to win the freedoms Great Britain denied them. On June 7, 1776, Richard Henry Lee of Virginia proposed a resolution to Congress. With a black handkerchief bandaging an injured hand, Lee rose and spoke the long-awaited—though for others long-dreaded—words. "That these United Colonies are, and of a right ought to be, free and independent states," proclaimed Lee. "They are absolved [released] from all allegiance to the British Crown, and that all political connection between them . . . is, and ought to be, totally dissolved."

John Adams leaped to his feet and seconded (approved) Lee's proposal. Through the day and into the night, Congress debated. The topic was too hot, too intense. They postponed making any decision. Instead, members appointed a committee of five to draft a paper, a declaration of independence. The committee included Virginian Thomas Jefferson, John Adams of Massachusetts, Benjamin Franklin of Pennsylvania, Roger Sherman from Connecticut, and Robert Livingston of New York.

The committee that wrote the Declaration of Independence is shown in this painting. The members are (**from left to right**) *Benjamin Franklin, Thomas Jefferson, Robert Livingston* (**seated, foreground**), *John Adams, and Roger Sherman.*

The main task of drafting the Declaration fell to lanky, red-haired Thomas Jefferson, aged thirty-three.

On July 1, Jefferson's draft declaration was ready to present to the Congress. With sweat beading every forehead in the steamy chamber of the Philadelphia State House, Congress debated the weighty issue of independence. John Dickinson, pale with anxiety, urged members to vote against independence. "Shall we destroy, in a moment of anger," he asked, the bonds and loyalties "cemented and tested by time?" Besides, it was too soon, Great Britain too strong, the colonies too weak, Dickinson protested. Proclaiming independence would be the same as destroying their homes in winter, before they had built another shelter.

The debate raged on. Congress deleted sections and added to Jefferson's document. Some southern delegates and New Englanders—who profited from the slave trade—opposed Jefferson's words condemning slavery as "a cruel war against human nature itself." For the sake of harmony, Congress scratched out that passage.

Late in the day, a raging storm battered the tall windows of the statehouse, mirroring the emotions inside. That evening Congress took a test vote. Pennsylvania, Dickinson's colony, voted against the resolution. South Carolina also voted no. Delaware's delegates stood divided. New York's delegates abstained from (held off) voting as they waited for instructions. Congress postponed the final vote until the next day, July 2. Those in favor of independence knew a unanimous vote was necessary—they must all stand together on this great and dangerous issue. Approval of the Declaration would certainly mean all-out war with Great Britain.

"THE GREATEST QUESTION WAS DECIDED"

The next day, John Dickinson and Robert Morris, who still felt their loyalty remained with Great Britain, could not in good conscience vote for independence. They chose not to vote on the issue, but the remaining Pennsylvania delegates voted yes. New York still abstained.

In this painting by John Trumbull, the Second Continental Congress ratifies (approves) the final draft of the Declaration of Independence on July 4, 1776.

South Carolina voted yes. Caesar Rodney of Delaware, sick with cancer, rode through the night to swing his colony's vote to yes. And so the deed was done. The colonies had broken their political ties with Great Britain. News of the momentous event leaked onto the streets. People clanged church bells and lit bonfires of celebration.

"Yesterday the greatest Question was decided," John Adams wrote to Abigail. He believed July 2 would be celebrated "from this time forward forever more" with parades and fireworks, sports, speeches, and ringing bells. He understood what the cost in toil and blood would be to "maintain this Declaration and support and defend these States . . . [but] I can see that the End is more than worth all the Means." On July 4, the Continental Congress formally approved the final version of the Declaration of Independence.

"The history of the present King of Great Britain is a history of repeated injuries" aimed at establishing "an absolute Tyranny over these states," wrote Jefferson in the Declaration. "To prove this let Facts be submitted to a candid world." He then laid out all the many reasons why the colonies should be independent states.

Jefferson's words declaring "All men are created equal" and entitled to "life, liberty, and the pursuit of happiness" lifted people's hearts. Still, as Jefferson labored over those words, the land he lived in allowed only white men who owned property to vote. No poor man could vote, no woman could vote, and nearly 500,000 African Americans lived as slaves with no rights at all. Native Americans weren't even considered citizens of the land they had occupied for centuries.

By July 5, the printer had copies of the Declaration to splash across Philadelphia. Meanwhile, riders galloped north and south carrying the news.

NEIGHBORS AMONG THE ENEMY

With the Declaration of Independence a fact of life, many places required citizens to take an oath of allegiance to the new United States. The Pennsylvania assembly claimed an oath was necessary to tell "our friends from our foes." Those who refused were marked as enemies. They could be threatened, lose their property, or worse, face arrest and a trial for treason. People who had hoped to sit out the war peacefully faced some tough decisions. Quakers and Moravians, whose religious beliefs didn't allow them to swear oaths, refused to swear allegiance. Some were fined and jailed. An anonymous Loyalist left a poem illustrating their plight.

> *The Cry was for Liberty—Lord what a Fuss!*
> *But pray, how much liberty left they for us?*

Perhaps half a million Americans remained loyal to the king. Many of these Loyalists aided the British any way they could. They joined the British military, formed militias, and passed information to British generals. They provided goods and money to support British troops. They hid spies and fugitives. Throughout the war, Loyalists passed counterfeit money to cripple the United States' fragile economy.

TORY ACT

Publifhed by Order of the Continental Congrefs, Philadelphia, Jan. 2, 1776.

WHEREAS it has been reprefented to this Congrefs, that divers honeft and well meaning, but uninformed people in thefe colonies, have by the art and addrefs of minifterial agents, been deceived and drawn into erroneous opinions, refpecting the American caufe, and the probable iffue of the prefent conteft.

Refolved, That it be recommended to the feveral Committees, and other friends to American liberty in the faid colonies, to treat all fuch perfons with kindnefs and attention, to confider them as the inhabitants of a country determined to be free, and to view their errors as proceeding rather from want of information, than want of virtue or public fpirit, to explain to them the origin, nature and extent of the prefent controverfy, to acquaint them with the fate of the numerous petitions prefented to his Majefty, as well by Affemblies as by Congrefes for reconciliation and redrefs of grievances, and that the laft from this Congrefs, humbly requefting the fingle favour of being heard, like all the others has proved unfuccefsful ; to unfold to them the various arts of adminiftration to enfnare and enflave us, and the manner in which we have been cruelly driven to defend by arms thofe very rights, liberties and eftates which we and our forefathers had fo long enjoyed unmolefted in the reigns of his prefent Majefty's predeceffors. And it is hereby recommended enabled with greater eafe and facility to carry this Refolution into execution. Refolved, That they be authorifed to call to their aid whatever Continental troops ftationed in or near their refpective colonies, may be conveniently fpared from their more immediate duty ; and the commanding officers of fuch troops are hereby directed to afford the faid Affemblies, Conventions, Committees or Councils of Safety, all fuch affiftance in executing this refolution as they may require, and which, confiftent with the good of the fervice, may be fupplied.

Refolved, That all detachments of Continental troops which may be ordered on the bufinefs in the aforegoing refolution mentioned, be, while fo employed, under the direction and controul of the Affemblies Conventions, Committees, or Councils of Safety aforefaid.

Refolved, That it be recommended to all the United Colonies to aid each other (on requeft from their refpective Affemblies Conventions Committees or Councils of fafety, and County Committees) on every emergency, and to cultivate, cherifh and increafe the prefent happy and neceffary union, by a continual interchange of mutual good offices.

And whereas the execrable barbarity with which this unhappy war has been conducted on the part of our enemies, fuch as burning our defencelefs towns and villages, expofing their inhabitants, without

While the Second Continental Congress was debating if the colonies should declare independence from Great Britain, the Congress passed the Tory Act in 1776. The act gave the Congress, American colonial governments, and militias the power to control Tories, or colonists loyal to the king and British Parliament.

Loyalist John Powers printed millions of dollars worth of fake bills and thought "he did the Crown a good service by that Work."

American Patriots saw Tories as the enemy who lived next door. Many families were torn apart because some members were Patriots and some Loyalists. Twenty-year-old Billy Silliman, a Patriot, described his Connecticut town as, "dark and gloomy indeed. . . . Our own countrymen & those whom we Valued as Friends are riseing against us." Billy's father, Gold Selleck Silliman, thought that people "who are at Bottom Friends to their Country" had brothers, sisters, sons, and fathers "among the Enemy [Tories]" and did not wish to see their relatives hurt.

Many Americans, particularly soldiers in battle, carried great bitterness toward Loyalists. Joseph Hodgkins, an American soldier, wrote his wife Sarah that a Tory "was Tried on Winsday [Wednesday] Condemed on thusday and Exicuted on Friday & I wish Twenty more whare sarved [were served] the same."

"THE DISTRESS OF THE INHABITANTS"

General Washington wondered where the British naval fleet would appear next after abandoning Boston. He decided that New York offered the British the greatest advantages and moved the Continental army south to meet them. In early July 1776, Howe's fleet arrived in New York Harbor from Nova Scotia. Howe landed nine thousand troops on Staten Island. More troops were sailing from Great Britain.

Washington had the newly adopted Declaration of Independence read to his gathered troops. Not far away, a cheering New York crowd pulled down a two-ton lead statue—covered in gold—of George III atop a horse. Billy Silliman, with the Patriot army, witnessed the event. He wrote his grandparents that "they talk of running his Majesty up into Bullets." Another man serving in the Massachusetts militia hoped the bullets made "from the Leaden George" would find targets in "his red-Coated and Torie Subjects."

By August nineteen thousand Continental and militia soldiers faced off against thirty-two thousand British and Hessian troops. One British official feared that the use of foreign troops "will tend to irritate and inflame the Americans" more than an army of British soldiers.

The sight of several hundred British ships massed in New York Harbor amazed Gold Selleck Silliman, a militia leader. The ships were so thick, he wrote, the masts looked like a forest. He hoped the outnumbered Americans could show the British that there was a difference between soldiers who only fight for pay and those that "fight for their Laws, their Liberties, their Wives & Children & everything else that is dear to them."

But the British captured Long Island, Brooklyn Heights, Manhattan, and Harlem Heights. Each time, the defeated colonial army retreated and regrouped. In New York, more than 1,300 overjoyed Loyalists sent congratulations to General Howe. A woman ripped down the rebel's flag and hoisted the king's banner.

The redcoats regarded the American soldiers with scorn. General Howe's private secretary, Ambrose Serle, claimed the Americans "will not fight at any Rate, unless they are sure of a Retreat. Their army is the strangest that ever was collected: Old men of 60, Boys of 14, and Blacks of all ages, and ragged for the most part, compose the motley Crew."

As time passed, both Loyalist and rebel citizens suffered in New York. Day and night, gunfire and cannon boomed across the city.

In this 1860 painting, men from the seagoing Marblehead Regiment silently transport Washington's troops to safety during the retreat from Long Island, New York, on the night of August 29, 1776. Outmanned and outpositioned, Washington decided to withdraw his men to fight another day.

Bodies lay scattered across pastures and fields. Sick troops infected the whole population. People ran out of food and other necessities, and it was difficult to get supplies through the battle lines. The price for everything skyrocketed. No one could afford to buy even basic needs. People fled the city in droves. New York's population plummeted from twenty-one thousand to five thousand.

British and Hessian soldiers were quartered with civilians. Lydia Post, a Long Island housewife, lost sleep, food, her fences, and then her cattle to the soldiers. Worse, the men barged about her home fighting. They played cards and dice all night, they drummed and danced and carried on, especially when fueled by their monthly ration of rum. And though the men treated her children kindly, she feared her youngsters would "contract evil" from the enemy soldiers.

This engraving from 1778 shows New York City ablaze in September 1776. While the origin of the citywide fire remains uncertain, the British believed colonial rebels started it by setting a series of small fires throughout New York. The British executed several men they claimed were responsible.

British soldiers treated few Americans, Loyalist or rebel, with respect. Women became the victims of rape. Upper-class females were off-limits, but soldiers considered women of the poorer classes easy targets. A man from Princeton, New Jersey, sadly reported how society treated rape victims. "Against both Justice and Reason We Despise these poor Innocent Sufferers," he wrote. Many women kept their ordeal "Secret for fear of making their lives miserable."

In the early hours of September 21, fanned by high winds, a fire quickly spread through parts of New York City. People stumbled into the streets—the old, the sick, women, and children—half dressed and running "they knew not where," wrote one witness. The crash of burning, falling houses, the shrieks and cries from parched throats filled the smoke-blackened night. Many people simply lay down in despair. About 1,100 houses burned.

The British, probably with reason, blamed the rebels for setting New York on fire to prevent the redcoats from occupying it. Loyalist Charles Stedman of Philadelphia reported that British soldiers arrested between "one and two hundred men and old women [who] were taken up during the night, and sent to gaol [jail] on suspicion," of helping set the blaze.

By late fall, Washington had retreated north of the city to White Plains. He then split his army between New York and New Jersey. Through battle and retreat, he struggled to keep an army in the field to face the British. But keeping soldiers in the American army became a battle worse than facing the enemy.

To all brave, healthy, able bodied, and well disposed young men..., who have the inclination to join the troops now raising under General Washington...
—Colonial army recruitment broadside, 1776

"THE RAGGED LOUSEY NAKED REGIMENT"

Drummers beat a lively step. Fifers added silver notes. An American officer marched through town holding high a banner that snapped in the breeze. People leaned against shop doorways. Some waved or cheered. The music announced an army recruiter, who called men and youths to join the fight for America's glorious cause. Teenage boys seeking adventure nudged one another in the ribs. "If you will enlist, I will," they said, egging each other on.

Half of America's population was under the age of sixteen. Recruiters targeted teenagers with patriotic speeches and songs. These young men had no wives, children, or property to worry about, and many dreamed of glory. Fifteen-year-old Joseph Plumb Martin told his grandparents he'd run away unless he could enlist. "The Americans were invincible [unbeatable] in my opinion," he recalled.

At first, Americans had fought the war using local militias. These farmers, shopkeepers, laborers, and apprentices trained near home, drilling under the eye of officers they'd elected. When danger threatened, militia soldiers dropped everything to defend their homes. When the crisis passed, the men returned to families, farms, and jobs. Thomas Paine summed up the trouble in *The American Crisis,* "I have always considered a militia as the best troops in the world for a sudden exertion, but they will not do for a long campaign."

Opposite: *New recruits to the Continental army march off to war. Colonial militia receive training from Baron von Steuben in 1777* (above). *While militia fought well against superior British forces early in the war, George Washington quickly saw that a trained and professional standing army was needed if the colonies were to have any chance against the British.*

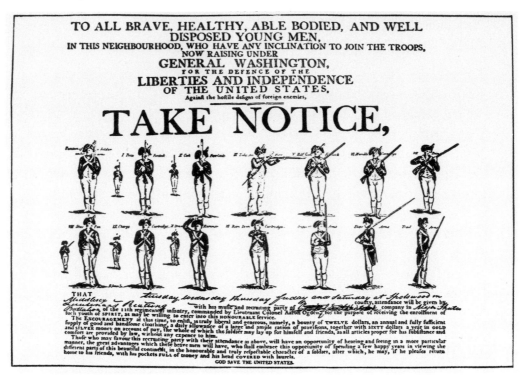

Broadsides like this one from 1776 asked able men to join George Washington and the Continental army "for the defence of the liberties and independence of the United States, against the hostile designs of foreign enemies." In return for service, the broadside promises a signing bonus, a salary, good food, and fine clothes.

"OUR MEN ENLIST VERY SLOW"

The colonies didn't have enough soldiers. Pressured by George Washington, Congress finally recognized that an army of come-and-go militia would not win the war. Nor could an army based on short one-year enlistments be counted on. At the end of 1775 and again in 1776, as most soldiers' enlistments ended, the men packed up and went home. The United States needed an army of long-term, well-trained soldiers. State militias could then provide support.

In September 1776, Congress voted to grant a twenty-dollar bonus, plus a new suit of clothes, to anyone who signed up for three years. Men who enlisted until the end of the war, whenever that might come, would also receive one hundred acres of land.

But many men, with families, with farms, with stores and businesses, would not sign on for three years. In 1777 the Congress ordered each state to sign on a certain number of soldiers. The states, in turn, held each of their towns responsible for their share. Many towns decided citizens would have no choice—they drafted men into the army. Other towns required men to enlist or send someone else to take their place. Draft letters made the situation crystal clear:

> *You are this evening drafted as one of the Continental men to go to General Washington's headquarters, and you must go or find an able bodied man in your [place], or pay a fine of twenty pounds . . . in twenty-four hours.*

Ebenezer Fox worked as a barber's apprentice. When Fox's master, John Bosson, received his draft letter, Bosson decided he no longer needed two apprentices. "If either of you had the spunk of a louse, you would offer to go for me," he told the boys. Ebenezer Fox took the barber's place in the draft. He knew Bosson was "a firm friend" to his country. But, said Fox, the idea of Bosson "shouldering a musket, buckling on a knapsack, leaving his quiet family, and marching several hundred miles for the good of his country, never took a place in his mind."

The *Connecticut Courant* reported in June 1777 that people "were busily employed in recruiting the children and servants of their neighbors, and forbidding their own to engage." The young and the poor, freedom fighters who did not qualify to vote, swelled the ranks of the Continental army.

"THEIR FREEDOM WITH THEIR MUSKETS"

Even though the British encouraged rebels' slaves to join the British army, Patriots at first rejected the idea of allowing African Americans to join the Continental army. About five thousand free African Americans, mostly from northern states, eventually served.

Some African American slaves went to war with their masters. A New Hampshire slave named Prince Whipple crossed the Delaware River with Washington's troops and surprised the British and Hessians at Trenton, New Jersey, on Christmas Day 1776.

But allowing slaves to enlist was a different matter. As only half of the expected white soldiers reenlisted at the end of 1775, thoughts slowly changed. Alexander Hamilton, a Patriot leader from New York, supported the idea of recruiting slaves. "I have not the least doubt, that the negroes will make very excellent soldiers," he wrote in March 1779. And if America does not use slaves for soldiers "the enemy probably will," Hamilton warned. Hamilton also recognized that "an essential part of the plan is to give them their freedom with their muskets." More than anything, the chance for freedom would secure the loyalty and courage of African American troops.

Even before Hamilton made his arguments, Rhode Island passed the Slave Enlistment Act in February 1778. After the British captured Newport, Rhode Island, the state struggled to fill its quota of soldiers. Every male slave who enlisted and received a mark of good health would be "immediately discharged from the service of his master or mistress, and be absolutely FREE."

The state arranged to pay slave owners for the loss of their property. A slave owner who freed a slave to fight was exempt from future military drafts. Many slave owners resisted, but some slaves negotiated with their masters—they'd go to war in the master's place in exchange for freedom. More than two hundred former slaves served in the all-black First Rhode Island Regiment. One white war veteran noted, "They were brave, hardy troops."

"HAPPY WHEN THEY GET RID OF US"

Financial troubles plagued the Continental army. The thirteen states, each guarding its own power, never granted Congress the means to raise taxes. Waging war cost huge sums of money. Washington's constant

pleas for food, clothing, more men, and supplies often went unan-
swered. Many congressmen felt the army should use force if necessary
and supply itself from surrounding farms. Washington tried to discour-
age this practice, not wishing to turn citizens away from the cause.

Food shortages loomed everywhere. Battles destroyed fields of
crops, and farmers off at war couldn't plant or harvest. Soldiers on
both sides spent more time seeking food than fighting battles. Both
armies foraged (searched) the countryside. Without paying or even
asking permission, they grabbed what they wanted from people's
barns and cellars. Ebenezer Fox and some camp mates killed a goose
with a stone and hid the dead bird inside a drum. The goose's owner

*A colonial woman defends her home against foraging British soldiers, killing
one. Soldiers from both sides took food, firewood, and whatever else they
needed from local people.*

complained bitterly to the commanding officer, but a search turned up gooseless. That night, reported Fox, their captain gobbled a juicy leg and wing, "without troubling us with any questions."

Not surprisingly, bitterness grew between soldiers and citizens. American troops felt neglected. It seemed to them that while they sacrificed all on their country's behalf, an ungrateful public starved them, withholding food or money to buy rations. Helpless civilians watched in distress and fury as armies stole their hay and bushels of cabbages and potatoes stored for winter. "How disgraceful . . . is it," asked Washington, "that the peaceable inhabitants, our countrymen and fellow citizens, dread our halting among them, even for a night and are happy when they get rid of us?"

In September 1777, the British seized Philadelphia, the capital city of the colonies. Robert Morton watched British and Hessian troops forage outside the city. The soldiers carted off wagonloads of fence posts, hay, vegetables, and animals. British commanders had promised to protect the king's loyal subjects and pay for their goods. But the soldiers did not know—or care—who was loyal. Many people, reported Morton, "are now entirely . . . ruined by the soldiers being permitted . . . to ravage and destroy their property." Many others, claimed Morton, would soon drop their Loyalist notions and "put themselves out of the British protection." Morton dug up and hid his own fences to prevent their use as British firewood.

"PINCHED WITH HUNGER"

During the long years of war, American soldiers suffered brutal hardships. Meager, rotten food led the list of miseries. "There comes a bowl of beef soup, full of burnt leaves and dirt," wrote Albigence Waldo. During the 1777–1778 winter camp at Valley Forge, Pennsylvania, Waldo cursed the commissary men, who purchased food for the troops. "May they [live] on Fire Cake [flour and water mush baked on hot rocks] & Water, 'till their glutted Gutts [full stomachs] are turned to Pasteboard," he wrote. Day after day, like a chorus of crows, the cry rose around the camp "No meat! No meat!"

Joseph Martin, a hardened war veteran at the age of sixteen, grumbled over a Thanksgiving feast in 1777: a bit of rice and a tablespoon of vinegar. He described himself as "pinched with hunger." During the winter camp at Morristown, New Jersey, in 1780, Martin wrote: "We were absolutely, literally starved." Martin joined others who gnawed bark from sticks and devoured roasted shoe leather. Officers, who lived slightly better, killed a pet dog and ate it.

GIVE ME SHELTER

On the march, soldiers slept in tents or under the stars. The ground underneath them was often wet or laced over with morning frost. On rainy nights, men gritted their teeth and got drenched to the bone. Blankets were rare. Joseph Martin lay on one side until "the upper side smarted with cold." Then he'd flip over and give the other side a turn. In summer men sagged beneath heat and humidity.

If the army planned to camp for a few weeks, soldiers built huts from stone, logs and branches, sailcloth—whatever they could lay their hands on. They helped themselves to saws and drills from citizens' barns. Officers usually paid for room and board at a local home. The armies did not fight in winter, and while the British stayed snug in cities such as New York or Philadelphia, the Americans froze and starved at such places as Valley Forge and Morristown.

NOT THE BEST DRESSED

Since Congress could barely feed the troops, they certainly didn't spend much on clothing. Most American soldiers had nothing like the sharp scarlet red uniforms of the British. Instead, they wore homespun cloth in browns and blues sewn into breeches and shirts. Wives used plant dyes to color their coats so each regiment had a variety of shades.

Colonial soldiers in ragged uniforms forage for firewood. General Washington feared that taking needed supplies from local people would turn them against the war effort. He pleaded with the Continental Congress to raise the money to properly equip and feed his men.

Most men wore long stockings and shoes made of cowhide. Few men owned boots. When the Patriot soldiers fought Loyalist militias, both sides were dressed in homespun, and it was hard to tell which side was which. American officers bought their own blue and buff uniforms.

Soldiers' letters home pleaded for shirts and socks. When Philadelphia women raised money for the cause, General Washington requested they make shirts for the troops. They supplied two thousand garments, each with the name of the sewer stitched inside.

Soldiers wore their clothes into rags. Garments danced with lice, fleas, and chiggers. These pests provided constant, itching misery. Some soldiers wore out their shoes and marched barefooted—even in snow. Many had only a ratty blanket to tie about their naked shoulders. Colonel Israel Angell's heart ached for his men as they marched through towns. Their "scandallous" appearance brought jeers from the citizens. "Ragged Lousey [covered with lice] Naked Regiment," people taunted the troops. "Such treatment" he wrote, "is discouraging and dispiriting."

MEDICAL CARE

Crowded conditions, contaminated food and water, filthy bodies, bedding, and clothing. These conditions spread smallpox, typhus, typhoid, and influenza among the army camps. Lack of vitamin C from fresh fruits and vegetables caused scurvy, which along with general malnutrition sickened the ranks. Ten to twenty men died of illness for every man killed by a British cannon or musket ball. Beginning in 1777, the army battled smallpox by inoculating the soldiers.

Medical knowledge of the era offered physicians few tools to fight disease or heal wounds. Wounds became tainted with infection from doctors, who had no notion that they needed to sterilize their knives or wash their hands to prevent infections. Amputating an infected limb most often spelled death for a soldier. The men lay packed into dirty hospitals, dying by the hundreds.

Doctors tried to set guidelines for cleaner camps, posting notices to air out blankets and burn used straw bedding. Benjamin Rush, a leading Philadelphia physician, published *Directions for Preserving the Health of Soldiers,* with advice on bathing, clothes, and healthy foods. But disease and poor medical care were the greatest cause of death.

"THE PRIVATES ARE ALL GENERALS"

Commanders complained about their liberty-minded soldiers. General Richard Montgomery fretted that his men "carry the spirit of freedom into the field, and think for themselves." In the heat of battle, soldiers needed to follow orders without question. Montgomery couldn't believe it when the men called "a sort of town meeting" to discuss his military plan. "The privates are all generals!" he declared with exasperation.

Washington's crackdown on discipline was aimed at men too "accustomed to unbounded freedom, and no control." Officers read the daily duty orders to the soldiers every morning after prayers. "Everyone is made to know his place and keep it," reported the Reverend William Emerson. A soldier who disobeyed orders faced whipping and possibly even death. The trouble was, just as one army settled into a disciplined fighting force, the men's terms of enlistment ran out. Another army had to be recruited, and the process started all over again.

MISSING HOME

Soldiers wrote home begging for news. Letters were slow in coming and often never arrived at all. General Nathanael Greene wrote his wife Catherine:

> *Could I have only a single line in return, to let me know you are well, it would afford me infinite pleasure. Nothing can exceed my anxiety to know your situation. . . . Pray be particular in giving an account of the Children. . . . These little anecdotes [stories] are pleasing.*

One night Albigence Waldo listened while a soldier in a nearby tent played a violin. The tender melody left Waldo in tears thinking of his wife, his children, and the warmth of his own fireside. He wished the music to stop, yet dreaded its stopping, for fear his sweet memories might vanish.

Often the Patriot soldiers received agonizing messages from home, begging them to return. Wives without money and food watched their children starve. Washington worried about wives coming to Valley Forge to plead with their husbands to come home. Eight to ten soldiers left the ranks for home each day.

Other families, especially the poor and homeless, attached themselves to the armies. Called camp followers, these women cooked, washed, nursed, and carried messages in return for half rations of food or a small payment. "The multitude of women . . . especially those who are pregnant, or have children, are a clog upon every movement," complained Washington.

American soldiers suffered greatly for the cause of liberty. They faced death or injury in battle. They hobbled through hundreds of miles of tedious marches. They shivered in camps made colder by empty stomachs. In December 1776, Thomas Paine paid eloquent tribute to these steadfast soldiers in *The American Crisis:*

> *These are the times that try men's souls: The summer soldier and the sunshine patriot will, in this crisis, shrink from the service of his country; but he that stands it now, deserves the thanks of man and woman.*

I want to have you come home & See us I look for you almost every day.
—Sarah Hodgkins, to her husband, away at war, 1776

"WHERE GOD, CAN WE FLY FROM DANGER?"

In March 1776, Mary Silliman of Connecticut wrote her parents: "What I have long feard is now come upon me." Her husband, Gold Selleck Silliman, had left with his militia regiment to defend New York. Her son Billy had gone too. Mary prayed that "the great happiness we have enjoyed may not end here."

Like thousands of other women, Mary plunged into her chores to silence fear and loneliness. The war created a staggering amount of work for women. Temperance Smith of Connecticut confessed that instead of "sending all my thoughts to heaven for the safety of my beloved husband and the salvation of our hapless country," she worried over chores. The basket of wool needed spinning, and the firewood must be chopped. The cloth steeping in the dying vat needed stirring. As her mind flicked through the day's chores, she wondered what she'd forgotten, "of the thousand [things] that must be done without fail."

KEEPING THE HOME FIRES BURNING

Most women worked from dawn into darkness, a round of chores from cooking and mending, to tending chickens and children. With goods in short supply or unavailable for any price, women also made cloth, soap, and candles—items they once might have purchased.

Towns expected women to sew shirts and coats for the local regiments. The women of Hartford, Connecticut, hand-stitched 1,000 coats and vests and 1,600 shirts. Women also tried to supply clothes and food for their soldier husbands. Sarah Hodgkins sent her husband and several male relatives shirts and socks. Mary Silliman made cheese and brewed cider for her husband, as well as making his clothes.

Society placed women on a rung below men. Legally, a wife disappeared into her husband's shadow. Each sex worked in its own sphere, and family financial matters belonged in a husband's hands. But with husbands gone, sometimes for years, wives faced running their homes on all fronts.

Timidly at first, then boldly, women stepped into their husbands' spheres. They hired help. They planted and harvested. They tended animals, mended tools and horse harnesses, and handled money and bookkeeping.

When a man first left, he often wrote home detailed letters about managing "my business" or "my farm." Men urged their wives to seek advice from male family members or friends. As wives learned to trust

Women, with the help of African American slaves, run a plantation in the southern colonies. During the American Revolution, many women took on the added responsibilities of running farms, plantations, and businesses while men were away fighting the war.

their own business sense, they wrote back about "our business" and "our farm." Eventually, fewer letters arrived home filled with advice. Many husbands even granted more control to their wives. William Palfrey added a P.S. to one letter for his wife Susannah: "I have altered my mind & made the Bills payable to you." Another husband wrote that his wife should "Apply [the money] as you think proper."

"SCENES OF WRETCHEDNESS"

Women were called upon to feed soldiers, house officers, and take in relatives fleeing the armies. They had to stretch every penny. Jean Blair took in twenty refuges. Her jam-packed home bustled with "continual confusion and not anything to eat but salt meat and hoe cake." From British-occupied Philadelphia in January 1777, teenager Deborah Norris wrote her friend Sally Wister. Sally's family had fled the city when the British arrived. "But alas! Our Philadelphia is not as it used to be," reported Deborah, ". . . soldiers are Quartered on private families. This is a great hardship. We have, as yet, escaped, and I hope we shall."

Wherever battles raged, women fled their homes in search of safety. The roads filled with women and children pushing carts jumbled with belongings. "Heavens! What a scene of wretchedness before this once happy and flourishing island!" wrote Mary Almy, as frightened people escaped Newport, Rhode Island, in 1778. Helena Brasher ran from a British attack on Esopus, New York. "Where God," she asked, "can we fly from danger? All places appear equally precarious."

A husband's death might mean his family ended up on the streets begging for food. Mary Donnelly's husband was lost at sea. She dreaded opening her eyes each morning to find her child crying for food "and not have it in my power to relieve him." At one point, Mary's first meal in three days, "was a morsel of dry bread and a lump of ice."

"Molly Pitcher" (above) *was a name awarded Revolutionary War heroines. The name is based on Mary Ludwig Hayes, who carried water to American soldiers, and then took her fallen husband's place loading cannons.*

It was no wonder that many women pleaded with their husbands not to reenlist when their time was up. Joseph Hodgkins felt a deep sense of duty to his country. But Sarah insisted he owed a greater duty to his family. He must find someone to take his place. "It will trouble me very much," she wrote him, "if you Should ingage again." Joseph returned home in the winter of 1776 but then reenlisted for another three years. When he left, Sarah was pregnant. She later wrote, she'd nothing to depend on except "troble & disapointments."

"CHANGING ONE MASTER FOR ANOTHER"

The British "have been tampering with our Negroes," wrote one slaveholder. The British encouragement to runaway slaves, first extended by Lord Dunmore, continued wherever the redcoat army marched. Furious white Patriots viewed British promises to free slaves as hypocrisy. Loyalists' runaway slaves were returned to their masters. Loyalist officers seized Patriots' slaves for their own plantations. Some escaped slaves were sent to labor on plantations in the Caribbean region. Loyalist official John Cruden commented:

> 'Tis only changing one master for another; let it be clearly understood that they are to serve the King for ever, and that those slaves who are not taken for his Majesty's service are to remain on the plantation, and Perform, as usual, the labor of the field.

But many enslaved African Americans only saw the chance for freedom. Two Georgia men informed John Adams that "the Negroes have a wonderfull Art of communicating Intelligence [news] among themselves. It will run severall hundreds of Miles in a Week or Fortnight." A British fleet off Cape Fear, North Carolina, found slaves coming from as far as 150 miles inland ready to join the British. Many African Americans weighed freedom against the risks of capture, starvation, uncertainty, and death, and still chose to run away.

A BLOODY FRONTIER

Although the war seemed centered in the East, frontier families weren't safe from its consequences. Most settlers lived on isolated farms. They were easy victims for a British tactic that sent Native American warriors to strike vulnerable settlements. In a proclamation issued June 1777, British general John Burgoyne made the threat clear. "I have but to give [word] to the Indian Forces under my direction, and they amount to Thousands, to overtake the hardened Enemies of Great Britain."

In this engraving from 1777, British general John Burgoyne meets Native Americans, hoping to create an alliance against the colonial rebels.

Colonel George Rogers Clark holds a meeting with Native Americans on the Western frontier during the 1770s in this nineteenth-century painting by Ezra Winter. Clark was able to negotiate a treaty of neutrality with many of the Indian peoples, robbing the British of allies in the West.

Patriots also sought Native American help, wooing tribes with free-flowing rum and promises of weapons and goods. The British, however, owned the advantage, for Native Americans had battled the land-hungry white colonists for generations. Not surprisingly, most tribes decided their best bet lay with the British. Mary Jemison, married to a Seneca man, reported that British agents promised that they "should never want for money or goods" as a reward for helping the king.

But not all tribes allied themselves with the British. White settlements surrounded the Catawba people living on the North and South Carolina borders. European diseases had brought many deaths and weakened the tribe. The Catawbas hoped to survive by supporting the Americans surrounding them. They served as scouts—gathering information on the Cherokee allies of the British—and helped fight the British at Savannah and Charleston.

The war split the Cherokee nation between generations. Younger warriors, who blamed the tribe's elders for selling away Cherokee lands, favored joining the British. It was "the intention of the white people to destroy [the Cherokee] from being a people," stated a young warrior named Dragging Canoe. British agent Henry Stuart fanned the flames of division. He assured the young men that the Americans had taken Cherokee lands against King George's wishes. The young warriors— well armed by the British—raided American settlements.

The American response was swift and brutal. "The Cherokee," wrote Thomas Jefferson, "will now be driven beyond the Mississippi" to show other tribes the consequence "of their beginning a war." Statesman Henry Laurens echoed Jefferson's sentiments. "If we succeed against the Cherokee," Laurens noted, "the Creek & other Indians may continue to be simple Spectators of our contest with Britain."

Six thousand men from Virginia, North Carolina, South Carolina, and Georgia destroyed Cherokee fields and burned towns in the fall of 1776. The assault reduced the Cherokee people to eating reptiles and insects. The tribe surrendered five million more acres of land to the new United States. The younger Cherokees moved west, hoping to continue the fight for their homelands.

Farther north, Joseph Brant was the leader of the Mohawk nation. He had been educated in white schools and had even traveled to London. Brant pushed the ancient Iroquois League to join the British. The Senecas, Onondagas, and Cayugas joined the Mohawks as British allies. The Oneidas and Tuscaroras leaned toward helping the Americans. In January 1777, the tribes met and extinguished their great council fire, the symbol of their unity. In the future, they would fight each other.

The British sent their Iroquois allies to raid white settlements on the New York, Pennsylvania, and Ohio Valley frontiers. Loyalists and Iroquois warriors hit the Wyoming Valley in Pennsylvania and the Mohawk Valley in New York in 1778. Hundreds of people died, their homesteads destroyed.

In autumn 1779, American general John Sullivan led a force of 4,500 men against Britain's Iroquois allies. They destroyed forty Native American towns, feasted on the Indian harvest, and burned what food they couldn't carry away—tens of thousands of bushels of corn, beans, and squash. Sullivan left the Native Americans with nothing to eat and winter only weeks away. "There is not a single town left in the country of the [Iroquois]," General Sullivan reported to the Congress.

The destruction of their towns made the Iroquois allies more dependent on Great Britain. Thousands moved to the British fort at Niagara, near the Canadian border.

A TURNING POINT AND DIPLOMACY

On October 17, 1777, British general John Burgoyne surrendered five thousand troops to American general Horatio Gates after the Battle of Saratoga in upstate New York. This major American victory

This 1817 painting by artist John Trumbull shows British general Burgoyne's surrender (left center) to American general Gates (center) following the Battle of Saratoga, New York. After a three-week engagement with the Continental army, Burgoyne surrendered his weakened army on October 17, 1777.

In this John Dunsmore painting, General Washington (left, on horseback) *and French nobleman Marquis de Lafayette* (right on horseback) *bolster troops at Valley Forge in early 1777. The French finally allied with the Americans about one year later. News of the alliance was a great relief to the battered colonial army.*

spurred France to recognize American independence. France offered money, troops, and supplies for the American cause. Benjamin Franklin and other American commissioners—who had been sent to Paris to persuade France to join the American cause—officially signed the alliance in February 1778.

Upon hearing news of the alliance, the American officers at Valley Forge cheered "loud huzzas" and drank to the health of French king Louis XVI, as once they'd saluted George III. "Triumph beamed" in every face, John Laurens, an officer with the Continental army, reported to his father.

For Loyalists, the opening months of 1778 seemed gloomy indeed. Just weeks before Saratoga, one New Jersey Loyalist had written, "The Force of the Rebellion is nearly spent . . . a Submission of the Colonies . . . may soon be expected." And then this!

Rumors flew that the new British commander, Sir Henry Clinton, planned to evacuate Philadelphia. Upper-class Loyalists had spent the British occupation of the city in a whirlwind of theater, concerts, and dances with British officers. Eighteen-year-old Rebecca Franks had delighted in her elegant gowns and male admirers. "No loss for partners," she assured her friends, "'tis a fix'd rule never to dance but two dances . . . with the same person." But they were abandoned and exposed "to the rage" of the rebels. Three thousand Loyalists sailed from Philadelphia with the British.

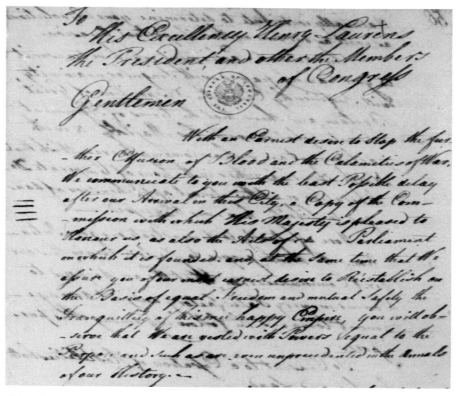

"Gentlemen, with an Earnest desire to stop the further Effusion [outpouring] of Blood and the Calamities of War, . . ." begins this 1778 letter from a British peace commission to the Continental Congress. Congress rejected the letter and the terms of peace it contained, settling for nothing less than independence.

"THE DOOR IS SHUT"

Britain hoped to undermine the American alliance with France. In June 1778, Britain sent a peace commission to Congress. The commissioners offered the Americans "a seat and voice in the Parliament of Great Britain." Trade and "mutual affection" would be restored. France meant only to "prevent our reconciliation, and to prolong this destructive war." The commission called the colonies "the British states throughout North America, acting with us in peace and war, under our common sovereign [king]."

But Britain refused to make the only offer Congress would now accept—to recognize American independence, then withdraw all troops. Henry Laurens noted that if Britain had earlier proposed "all the fine things now offered," the people of America would "joyfully have embraced that proposition. . . . But now . . . the Door is shut."

James Parker, a Norfolk Loyalist, called the commission "humiliating." He wrote, "Low is the dignity of G.B. [Great Britain] fallen indeed," begging for hearings "from her Rebellious subjects." A few days later, Britain declared war on France.

The Revolution was in the minds and hearts of the people.
—*John Adams, 1818*

"THE REVOLUTION JUST ACCOMPLISHED"

People in Boston, Newport, New York, and Philadelphia had endured destruction of life and property. Like a windblown fire, the war spread from eastern cities to frontier outposts. Then, in 1778, the British turned their attention to the southern states.

They captured Savannah, Georgia, in December 1778. Stephen De Lancey, a New York Loyalist officer, found the people pale and sickly. The slaves, whose labor provided crops of rice and sugar, were nearly naked "and are very disgusting to the Eye. . . . At what an expense of life and Happiness do we eat Rice and Sugar!" he wrote his wife.

Charleston, South Carolina, fell in May 1780, after a two-month siege. The southern department of the Continental army surrendered about five thousand soldiers and militia. Perhaps twenty thousand South Carolina slaves escaped to the British. Redcoat officers used the slaves as carpenters, blacksmiths, road builders, cooks, and trench diggers.

All over the South, enslaved people took advantage of wartime chaos and British offers of freedom. Eliza Pinckney of South Carolina complained that her slaves considered themselves "perfectly free" and "quite their own masters." One British general noticed that wherever the redcoats advanced, "all negroes, men, women, and children . . . thought themselves absolved from all respect to their American masters."

Opposite: *a Patriot flag from the Revolution. The coiled snake and "Don't Tread on Me" battle slogan asserts the will of the colonials to strike back at the control of Great Britain. "Cornwallis has overrun the whole country. . . ," writes Thomas Jefferson on May 28, 1780, in his "State of Things at Charleston." Charleston, South Carolina, fell to British commander Lord Cornwallis that month.*

This British political cartoon of the 1780s shows American colonists as "savages" (Native Americans) brutally attacking Tories during the Revolution. "Britannia" (far right), *a symbol of Great Britain, lashes out at members of Parliament for doing nothing to stop the bloodshed.*

"THE PEOPLE HAVE BECOME . . . SAVAGE"

The face of war wore a grisly new mask in the South. Regular citizens joined both Loyalist and rebel militias in raiding, plundering, and murdering one another. People used the war as an excuse to pay back old grudges against neighbors. "The people," wrote William Pierce, "have become perfectly savage."

Patriots practiced what teenager James Collins called "ferreting out the Tories." Under cover of darkness, Patriots smashed in the door of a suspected Loyalist's home and rushed inside brandishing swords. They dragged terrified inhabitants from under beds and out of corners. As the Loyalist family cowered, pleading for their lives, the Patriots slashed, shattered, and ripped their house apart. Most felt the Loyalists reaped what they deserved. Collins of South Carolina was a good horseman who rode "as a collector of news" for the Americans. "There were none of the poor fellows much hurt," he noted after one raid, "only they were hacked about their heads and arms enough to bleed freely."

People felt unsafe sleeping in their own beds. Hundreds hunkered down in woods or in swamps. They hid their furniture and buried their possessions. "If a woman had but one quart of salt, to salt mush for her children, or a spoon to sup it with, she must keep it hid," reported Collins. Many citizens switched sides, taking oaths of allegiance to save their lives.

The devastation of the South Carolina countryside shocked American general William Moultrie. "The squirrels and birds of every kind were totally destroyed," he wrote. "No living creature was to be seen." In October 1780, Washington named General Nathanael Greene commander of the army's southern department. Greene wrote his wife: "You can have no idea of the distress and misery that prevails here. Hundreds of families . . . are now reduced to beggary and want."

James Collins fought in militia skirmishes and at the battle of Kings Mountain, South Carolina, in October 1780. At Kings Mountain, he joined with one thousand other backcountry Patriots to fight an equal number of Loyalists under British commanders.

Under pressure from a scornful mob of colonists, a Tory signs his name to the Patriot cause in this British political cartoon from the late 1700s. Threatened with imprisonment, beatings, tarring and feathering, and even hanging, citizens from both sides of the conflict chose to switch sides to save their lives.

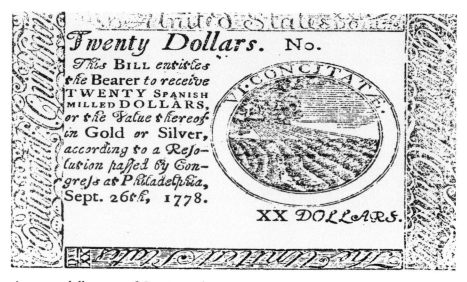

A twenty-dollar note of Continental currency, printed in 1778. The Continental Congress authorized the printing of currency to pay war expenses. More money was printed than there was gold or silver to back it, making the currency worthless.

The Loyalists, penned in on all sides, surrendered. The next morning, wrote Collins, "The scene became really distressing; the wives and children of the poor Tories came in, in great numbers. Their husbands, fathers, and brothers, lay dead in heaps, while others lay wounded or dying." Collins and his father each helped themselves to a horse, guns, clothing, and ammunition—and went home.

"YOU THAT HAVE MONEY"

As the war went on, a nearly bankrupt Congress kept printing stacks of paper money to pay expenses. By 1780 so much paper money was in circulation that its worth fell to a fraction of the face value. Matters worsened as wartime shortages sent prices soaring.

Merchants and farmers refused to accept the nearly worthless paper money. They demanded hard money, gold or silver coins. People with hard money paid the high prices, making the paper money in people's pockets as valuable as oak leaves. It required nearly $2,934 in paper bills to equal $100 in coin.

One broadside posted around Pennsylvania declared: "In the midst of money we are in poverty, and exposed to want in a land of plenty. You that have money...down with your prices, or down with yourselves."

Abigail Adams reported an incident of a greedy Boston merchant selling coffee for extravagant prices. Nearly one hundred women seized the merchant, snatched his keys, opened his warehouse, and carried off his coffee. A large flock of gentlemen "stood amazed silent Spectators."

MUTINY IN THE RANKS

Everyone felt the pinch, but soldiers felt it worst of all. They were paid in paper money. The money they had been promised when they enlisted had little buying power. Many soldiers received no pay at all. One officer, Ebenezer Huntington, unpaid for six months, claimed, "I despise my Countrymen....I am in Rags...and all this for my cowardly countrymen [who] hold their Purse Strings...rather than part with a Dollar to their Army."

In January 1781, some Pennsylvania troops in New Jersey had had enough. The men raided weapon stores and killed several officers. Then they marched out in formation, heading to confront the Congress in Philadelphia.

A few days later, Washington wrote, "The event, which I have long dreaded would be the consequence of keeping the Army without pay, Cloathing, and [frequently without] Provision, has at length come to pass." An army ran on discipline—mutiny had to be punished.

Washington sent New Jersey troops and militia to stop the mutineers. "Grant no terms," ordered Washington, "while they are...in a state of resistance." He reminded the militia's citizen-soldiers that liberty could not exist with "armed soldiers dictating terms to their country."

Seven of the mutineers were executed in May 1781. Officers marched their regiments past the scene. "This was an awful exhibition," wrote soldier Ebenezer Denny, "the seven . . . were seen by the troops just as they had sunk or fell under the fire. The sight must have made an impression on the men; it was designed with that view."

"THE WORLD TURNED UPSIDE DOWN"

Washington held his army together. In August 1781, he heard news that actually made the general jump for joy—a French fleet would soon arrive in the Chesapeake Bay. Washington hurried the army south from New York to his home state of Virginia. There they faced the British army under Lord Charles Cornwallis.

For several weeks in October 1781, cannons boomed across Yorktown, Virginia. Beneath people's feet, the streets shuddered. Heaps of shot and cannonballs littered the town. Once fine houses lay shattered, piles of wood, brick, and glass. At night mortar shells arched across the inky sky, trailing fire in a brilliant and horrifying spectacle.

African American slaves had flocked to Cornwallis. When Britain's food supplies dwindled, the African Americans were driven out from behind

A British warship sinks into Chesapeake Bay during a battle with the French navy in 1781. The French sealed the bay, pinning Cornwallis at Yorktown and cutting his supply line.

British lines. Starving and sick with smallpox, they died around York-town in great numbers. Thomas Jefferson estimated that Virginia "lost under Lord Cornwallis's hands . . . about 30,000 slaves, and that of these about 27,000 died of the small pox and camp fever."

Josiah Atkins, a Connecticut blacksmith, found Virginia "vastly different" from his part of the world. "Some men in these parts, they tell Me . . . have two or 3 hundred . . . slaves." To Atkins it seemed strange, indeed, that men "who pretend to stand for the *rights of mankind* for the *liberties of society,* can delight in oppression, & that even of the worst kind!"

At Yorktown, in long rows of trenches, American and French soldiers faced the British troops. The French fleet in Chesapeake Bay bottled up any British escape by sea.

On October 17, American soldiers, deafened by the constant firing, spied the red coat of a British drummer atop the trench across the way. An officer, waving a white handkerchief of surrender, climbed out of the British trenches. An American officer raced across to meet him and accompanied the man to a house near the rear of the lines. Guns stopped firing and crowds of soldiers, British, American, and French, crammed onto the mounds of earth and studied each other.

Two days later, seven thousand British soldiers surrendered to George Washington. The British military band played "The World Turned Upside Down" as redcoats marched between long lines of American troops. This seemingly topsy-turvy world "was too pleasing to an American," wrote Patriot soldier St. George Tucker. Cornwallis claimed illness and did not attend the surrender.

Americans celebrated the Yorktown victory with torchlight parades and attacks on Tory homes. Frantic Loyalists, like John Hamilton of Charleston, still hoped for a British victory. "The last man and shilling [British coin] must be expended before she [Britain] gives America her independence." But others felt the end approaching. The drain on Britain's treasury and the great loss of men had sucked the desire to fight out of many in Great Britain.

These are the opening lines of General Washington's Articles of Capitulation (surrender) to Lord Cornwallis. With Cornwallis trapped and outnumbered at Yorktown, Washington firmly offered his terms in October 1781.

In February 1782, lawmakers in the British House of Commons voted not to continue the war in America. Peace negotiations with American commissioners in France began that spring.

THE BLESSINGS OF PEACE

In Paris on November 30, 1782, Benjamin Franklin, John Adams, John Jay, and Henry Laurens signed a preliminary peace treaty with Britain. Great Britain recognized American independence. The new country's borders stretched west to the Mississippi River and from the Great Lakes in the North to the 31st parallel in the South (just below present-day Jacksonville, Florida). Congress was to recommend that state lawmakers restore the property and rights of Loyalists. The treaty meant to assure that Loyalists were protected from "any future

Loss or Damage, either in his Person Liberty or Property." The commissioners signed the final treaty in September 1783. "I hope it will be lasting," wrote Franklin, "for in my opinion, there never was a good war or a bad peace."

But signatures upon paper could not blot out years of anger and humiliation. While many Americans wished to put the war behind them, others could not forgive Loyalists or rebels. "The spirit of persecution and violence against the unhappy loyalists does not appear to abate," wrote Loyalist David Colden of New York. Worse, "The people have been taught a dangerous truth, that all power is derived from them." Colden saw only chaos ahead. Another New York Loyalist noted, "The mob now reigns" just as at the beginning. Many believed that monarchy must return, for the new American government, a loose organization of the states under the Articles of Confederation, could not possibly last more than four or five years.

While most Loyalists wished to stay in America, an estimated 80,000 to 100,000 left with the British during and after the war. In July 1782, the British left Savannah. They sailed from Charleston in December. The last British troops withdrew from New York in November 1783. Tens of thousands of Loyalists and African Americans, many of them the slaves of Loyalists, sailed too. They overflowed Nova Scotia and pushed into other parts of Canada. Loyalists emigrated to Great Britain and British colonies in the Caribbean. As Nancy Jean Cameron's Loyalist family prepared to leave for a Canada home, she wrote a cousin:

> The long weary years of war, followed by the peace years, that have been to us worse than the time of fighting, are over. Our lands are confiscated and it is hard to raise money . . . the children little realize the days of hardship before them. . . . When I leave this beautiful Mohawk Valley and the land that I had hoped we would always hold I shall hear no more the bitter label, "Tory."

This American antislavery broadside dates from the late 1700s. It asks colonial Patriots to apply their principles of freedom to the cause of the enslaved in America. Many African Americans petitioned Congress and local governments for the abolition [outlawing] of slavery during and after the Revolution. Slavery in the new nation, however, would flourish for another eighty years.

"ONE PRICELESS GEM"

An estimated 100,000 slaves escaped during the war, but many died of disease or hunger, never tasting real freedom. Some won freedom fighting for British or American forces. Elleanor Eldridge wrote that her father, an American soldier, was left with only worthless continental money for his service, but he'd earned "one priceless gem, LIBERTY." Nearly 3,000 former Loyalist African American soldiers, called the Black Pioneers, settled in Nova Scotia in 1783.

Some masters conveniently forgot promises of liberty made years before. Ned Griffen, who'd fought in his master's place in exchange for freedom, petitioned the North Carolina assembly for his rights in April 1784. The legislators declared that Griffen "in every respect declared a freeman, and he shall be . . . forever delivered . . . from the yoke of slavery."

Many African Americans freed by the war devoted their lives to the cause of liberty and equality. Some spent years petitioning for an end to slavery. Others lobbied state legislatures about ending the slave trade or tried to protect escaped slaves from their masters. Some free blacks saved for years to buy freedom for family members still in bondage.

The Revolution changed slavery forever in the northern states. The war cry that called for liberty and the natural rights of human beings struck a chord with many. Enslaved labor had never driven the northern economy as it did the large plantation economy of the South. Many states began a gradual abolition of slavery. In Pennsylvania all children born into slavery after 1780 become free at the age of twenty-eight. Rhode Island freed female slaves at eighteen and male slaves at twenty-one. By 1810 nearly 75 percent of African Americans in northern states lived as free people.

The southern economy, based on large cash crops such as tobacco and rice, relied upon enslaved labor. In the years after the war, the slave system grew more oppressive. Western lands opened by the peace treaty beckoned American settlers, who surged into Kentucky, Tennessee, Mississippi, and Alabama. Many brought their slaves with them.

"WE THE INDIANS"

It had taken white colonists 150 years to reach from the seacoast to the Appalachian Mountains. Within a single decade, Americans would settle an equally large area of land west of the mountains, as pioneers swarmed west. The British had handed over the homelands of their Native American allies to the Americans. Mohawk chief Kanonraron declared that his people had been the king's allies—not his subjects. He blasted the betrayal as "an act of Cruelty and Injustice."

The war robbed Native Americans of land, food, and resources. They could not stand against the sheer numbers of white Americans, wave upon wave of people, flooding their tribal homelands.

Thayendanegea (Joseph Brant), a Mohawk leader who allied with the British during the Revolution. Following the war and without a British ally, he observed that his people's situation was dangerously uncertain.

Nations that had aided the Americans, such as the Catawba, found some reward. About forty men received pay for their services, and after a Catawba petition to the government, they were allowed to hunt on white-owned lands that had once belonged to them.

The British did grant the Iroquois nations a tract of land in Canada. A few years after the war, Mohawk chief Joseph Brant reflected sadly on the unsettled situation. "The Yankys [Americans] are taking advantage all the while and our friends the English seems getting tired of us."

LIKE OLD WORN-OUT HORSES

An estimated twenty-five thousand Americans died during the war—in battle, from disease, and from hunger. In terms of today's population, that would equal more than two and a half million war casualties. Soldiers who survived the war felt ill-used. Joseph Martin, who signed on as a lad seeking adventure, summed it up. "When the country had drained the last drop of service it could screw out of the poor soldiers, they were turned adrift like old worn-out horses." Congress had no way to pay the soldiers or honor past promises of pension pay.

In March 1783, an unsigned letter circulated through the army camps. The author urged soldiers to either "Go, starve, and be forgotten!" or instead seek revenge on a country that ignored and insulted her heroes.

Washington pleaded with men and officers to remain calm and not make this dreadful choice. Do not overturn "the liberties of our Country," he urged. Do not "open the flood Gates of Civil discord. . . . My God! What can this writer have in view?"

Washington petitioned Congress on behalf of the army. He sent letters to the individual states. And he urged people to give the U.S. government enough power to fulfill the nation's debt to the soldiers. But at the time, his efforts brought little result. Eventually, some veterans received land and pensions for war injuries.

THE LIGHT OF THE REVOLUTION

The war demanded sacrifice and action from nearly every person in Revolutionary America. People of all classes raised their voices. Common citizens, including those usually ignored by politicians,

This excerpt from the Journals of Congress *contains a part of* General Washington's *response to the anonymous writer who urged* Continental *soldiers, in 1783, to "go, starve, and be forgotten" or to seek revenge against the American government that had forgotten them.*

308	*Journals of Congress*

be compelled into instant compliance, has something so shocking in it, that humanity revolts at the idea. My God! what can this writer have in view, by recommending such measures? Can he be a friend to the army? Can he be a friend to this country? Rather is he not an insidious foe? Some designing emissary, perhaps, from New York, plotting the ruin of both, by sowing the seeds of discord and separation between the civil and military powers of the continent? and what a compliment does he pay to our understandings, when he recommends measures, in either alternative impracticable in their nature? But, here, gentlemen, I will drop the curtain, because it would be as imprudent in me to assign my reasons for this opinion, as it would be insulting to your conception to suppose you stood in need of them. A moment's reflection will convince every dispassionate mind of the physical impossibility of carrying either proposal into execution. There might, gentlemen, be an impropriety in my taking notice, in this address to you, of an anonymous production; but the manner in which that performance has been introduced to the army, the effect it was intended to have, together with some other circumstances, will amply justify my observations on the tendency of that writing.

rushed to the streets in protest. They boycotted goods to change laws. They signed petitions and penned lists of grievances. Everywhere, Americans debated political ideas.

Yet the notion stated in the Declaration of Independence that all people are "created equal . . . with certain unalienable Rights" remained a new concept for many. People were used to kings, gentlemen of good fortunes, and ladies of the highest rank set above common folk. They were used to masters ruling over servants, and men over women. But the Revolution created unrest and a desire for change, which continued after the war ended.

The shining goals of the Revolution, the light of equality and liberty, remained alive as cornerstones in the new nation's story. In years to come, Americans fighting for the end of slavery, for women's rights, and for civil rights, illuminated the Revolution's words and ideals for new generations.

General Washington (front, center) *resigns from the army before the Congress at Annapolis, Maryland, in 1783 in this 1817 painting by John Trumbull.*

On December 23, 1783, at Annapolis, Maryland, George Washington resigned from the military during a public ceremony before the Congress. The general gripped his resignation letter in both hands, but still the paper trembled. He paused but could not quite master his voice, which quivered as he asked God to watch over the new nation. Congressmen and spectators wept openly.

James McHenry, surgeon, soldier, and congressman, wrote his wife of the day's event. Like many Americans, McHenry's thoughts dwelt on "the Revolution just accomplished—the new situation into which it had thrown the affairs of the world—the past—the present—the future."

A new day had dawned. New challenges lay ahead.

THE VETERANS' PREDICAMENT

Be patient, Congress said, repeatedly stalling soldiers' complaints about their lack of pay. The U.S. government feared uprisings among the disgruntled soldiers. During 1783 regiments were disbanded in stages to prevent a mass of angry troops freed from duty at one time. Washington wrote the men were sent home "goaded by a thousand things" promised and never delivered by the government.

Soldiers waited years for their back pay, and as time went by, many turned bitter toward their government. Many veterans suffered chronic health troubles from their years of hardship. Joseph Hodgkins' brave patriotism sank into disappointment. He felt he'd received nothing from his country, not even thanks. The nation "will Ever Be guilty of Ruening [ruining] thousands [of men] unless they Due [do] something more for them then what they Ever have Done yet," he wrote. So many veterans needed jobs that employers could offer low wages and still find workers.

Instead of pay, the U.S. government mainly offered soldiers titles to frontier lands. Land was one thing of some value the new nation had plenty of—ten million acres were set aside for veterans. But Joseph Plumb Martin wrote later that most soldiers were never told what to do to get their lands. There were no agents or government officials to see to it that soldiers received their portion of the set-aside land. Hungry land investors, called speculators, offered soldiers a fraction of what the land was really worth. Many soldiers sold their land just to get money for the journey back home from the war.

Some veterans eventually received land. Virginia used land claims in Ohio (statehood,1803) to pay its war veterans. In 1820, thirty-seven years after the war, Georgia allowed veterans to enter a land lottery. In the 1830s, Massachusetts awarded veterans land in Maine (statehood, 1820).

Not until 1818 did Congress finally authorize monthly pensions for veterans. But without faxes, phones, e-mail, or quick transportation, it was difficult for veterans to unearth and present old documents proving where they had served and under which officer. Without proof, the government denied petitions for pensions. Many veterans had died before they had a chance to apply, though their widows could still apply and receive a share of the money owed their husbands. According to the Department of Veterans Affairs, the last surviving soldier of the American Revolution died in 1869 at the age of 109. His name was Daniel F. Bakeman.

The war's most famous soldier was the army's commander, George Washington. At the time, many politicians feared Washington would use his angry army and seize power, setting himself up as a military dictator or king. But Washington resigned from the army in December 1783 and petitioned the government to grant benefits to his former soldiers. His action assured that the new nation would have a civil, not a military, government. Six years later, from 1789 to 1796, Washington served as the nation's first president.

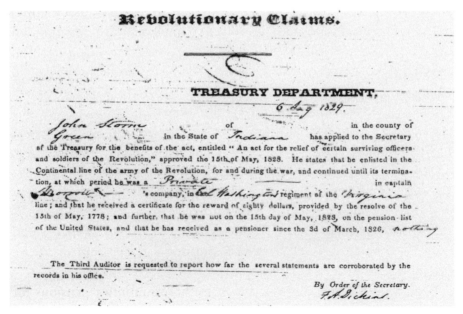

An ancestor of the author, John Storm served as a private in the Virginia Regiment of the Continental army from 1780 to 1783. He submitted this petition for pension pay in 1829.

DRAFTING THE DECLARATION

On the second floor of a brick boarding house, Thomas Jefferson rose early, sipped tea, ate biscuits, and for two weeks, composed one of the most important documents in American history. Jefferson wrote with a quill feather pen sharpened with a small knife and dipped into ink. He sat at a portable desk of his own design. As his quill scratched across the paper (see draft, facing page), Jefferson must have wondered if he'd end up dangling from a tree, hanged as a traitor.

Jefferson wrote, revised, and polished, carefully considering every word. He drew inspiration from English political philosopher John Locke (1632–1704) as well as from American writings like *Common Sense* and the Virginia Declaration of Rights. After several drafts, he asked John Adams and Benjamin Franklin for suggestions. The only known copy of Jefferson's rough drafts is preserved in the Library of Congress (for more fragments, visit http://memory.loc.gov/ammem/mdbquery.html, search term "Declaration draft").

The Declaration of Independence stands as a monument of political ideals. It states that people have natural rights to "life, liberty, and the pursuit of happiness," and that governments only govern with the consent of their citizens. Jefferson listed the Declaration as one of his proudest achievements.

During the Revolution, Congress carried the Declaration with other government papers as they fled British troops. A clerk hid the document during the War of 1812 (1812–1815) when the British burned Washington, D.C. In the mid-1800s, the Declaration was exposed to damaging sunlight as it hung in the Patent Office Building in Washington, D.C. During World War II (1939–1945), the government stashed the Declaration with the country's gold supply at Fort Knox in Kentucky.

You can view the Declaration of Independence today (alongside the United States Constitution and the Bill of Rights) in the National Archives in Washington, D.C. The fragile documents rest beneath bullet-proof glass filled with special gas and enough humidity to preserve the old parchments. Each night the documents are lowered into a concrete and steel vault for safe keeping.

A Declaration by the Representatives of the UNITED STATES OF AMERICA, in General Congress assembled.

When in the course of human events it becomes necessary for one people to dissolve the political bands which have connected them with another, and to assume among the powers of the earth the separate and equal station to which the laws of nature & of nature's god entitle them, a decent respect to the opinions of mankind requires that they should declare the causes which impel them to the separation.

We hold these truths to be self-evident; that all men are created equal & independent, that from that equal creation they derive rights inherent & inalienable, among which are the preservation of life, & liberty, & the pursuit of happiness; that to secure these ends, governments are instituted among men, deriving their just powers from the consent of the governed; that whenever any form of government shall becomes destructive of these ends, it is the right of the people to alter or to abolish it, & to institute new government, laying it's foundation on such principles & organising it's powers in such form, as to them shall seem most likely to effect their safety & happiness. prudence indeed will dictate that governments long established should not be changed for light & transient causes: and accordingly all experience hath shewn that mankind are more disposed to suffer while evils are sufferable, than to right themselves by abolishing the forms to which they are accustomed. but when a long train of abuses & usurpations [begun at a distinguished period, &] pursuing invariably the same object, evinces a design to reduce them under absolute Despotism, it is their right, it is their duty, to throw off such

SOURCE NOTES

p. 6 Richard Morris, ed. *The American Revolution, 1763–1783: A Bicentennial Collection of Documents* (Columbia: University of South Carolina Press, 1970), 89–90.

p. 6 Ibid., 167.

p. 7 *British Historical Documents: Proclamation of Rebellion, 1775,* 2004, http:// www. Britannia.com/history/docs/procreb.html (May 2003).

p. 9 Ibid.

p. 10 Morris, 14.

p. 11 Ibid., 18.

p. 12 Jared Ingersoll, quoted in Morris, 65.

p. 13 Ibid.

p. 13 Morris, 192.

p. 14 Ibid., 72.

p. 14 Ibid., 74.

p. 15 Ibid., 77.

p. 15 Ibid.

p. 15 Ibid., 89–90.

p. 16 Ray Raphael, *A People's History of the American Revolution: How Common People Shaped the Fight for Independence* (New York: The New Press, 2001), 19.

p. 16 Ibid., 24.

p. 16 Morris, 80.

p. 17 Ibid., 98.

p. 19 Ibid., 27.

p. 20 Ibid., 28.

p. 20 Ibid., 43.

p. 21 Ibid., 109.

p. 21 Ibid., 104.

p. 22 Raphael, 111.

p. 22 William Tennent III, quoted in Mary Beth Norton, *Liberty's Daughters: The Revolutionary Experience of American Women, 1750–1800* (New York: HarperCollins, 1980), 159.

p. 23 Ibid., 160.

p. 23 Raphael, 18.

p. 25 Catherine Crary, ed., *The Price of Loyalty: Tory Writings From the Revolutionary Era* (New York: McGraw-Hill, 1973), 16.

p. 26 Ibid., 25.

p. 26 Ibid., 22.

p. 27 Raphael, 43.

p. 27 Ibid., 45.

p. 28 Crary, 27.

p. 28 Ibid., 28.

p. 29 Morris, 134.

p. 29 Ibid., 138.

p. 29 Norton, 158.

p. 30 Raphael, 324.

p. 30 Ibid., 171.

p. 31 Ibid., 38.

p. 31 Ibid., 37.

p. 31 Ibid., 27.

p. 31 Christopher Gadsden, quoted in Raphael, 109.

p. 31 Ibid., 108.

p. 31 Norton, 170.

p. 32 Herbert Aptheker, ed. *A Documentary History of the Negro People in the United States* vol. 1 (New York: Citadel, 1951), 7.

p. 32 Raphael, 292.

p. 33 Ibid., 298.

p. 34 John Rhodehamel, comp., *The American Revolution, Writings from the War of Independence.* (New York: The Library of America, 2001), 23.

p.35 Ibid., 19.

p.36 Ibid., 62.

p. 36 Ibid., 15.

p. 36 Ibid., 28.

p. 37 Ibid., 25.

p. 37 Ibid., 21.

p. 38 Crary, 35.

p. 38 Rhodehamel, 53.

p. 38 Raphael, 129.

p. 39 Crary, 34.

p. 39 Morris, 215.

p. 39 Rhodehamel, 20.

p. 39 Ibid., 37.

p. 40 Richard Buel and Joy Buel, *The Way of Duty: A Woman and Her Family in Revolutionary America* (New York: W. W. Norton, 1984), 97.

p. 41 Rhodehamel, 41.

p. 41 Ibid., 34.

p. 42 Ibid., 65.

p. 42 Ibid.

p. 42 Ibid., 66.

p. 42 Morris, 164–165.

p. 43 Joseph Fields, comp., *Worthy Partner: The Papers of Martha Washington* (Westport, CT: Greenwood Press, 1994), 164.

p. 43 Rhodehamel, 55.

p. 43 Ibid., 56.

p. 43 Ibid., 58.

p. 44 Ibid., 59.

p. 44 Raphael, 195.

p. 44 Ibid.

p. 44 Ibid.

p. 45 Ibid., 247.

p. 45 Rhodehamel, 85.

p. 45 Ibid., 133.

p. 45 Raphael, 259.

p. 46 Rhodehamel, 127.

p. 47 Thomas Paine, *Common Sense,* quoted in Morris, 176.

p. 47 Ibid., 182.

p. 47 Ibid., 180.

p. 48 Ibid., 181.

p. 48 Ibid., 86.

p. 49 Ibid., 206.

p. 49 Ibid., 207.

p. 49 Ibid., 208.

p. 49 Crary, 125.

p. 50 John Bowater, quoted in Rhodehamel, 114.

p. 50 Crary, 126.

p. 51 Morris, 216.

p. 51 David McCullough, *John Adams* (New York: Simon and Schuster, 2001), 118.

p. 52 William Dudley, ed., *The American Revolution, Opposing Views* (San Diego: Greenhaven Press, 1992), 134.

p. 53 Rhodehamel, 125.

p. 53 Ibid., 127.

p. 54 Raphael, 170.

p. 55 Crary, 385.

p. 55 Buel and Buel, 111.

p. 55 Gold Selleck Silliman, quoted in Buel and Buel, 133–134.

p. 56 Raphael, 172.

p. 56 Billy Silliman, quoted in Buel and Buel, 100.

p. 56 Rhodehamel, 132.

p. 56 Ambrose Serle, quoted in Rhodehamel, 196.

p. 56 Gold Selleck Silliman, quoted in Buel and Buel, 113.

p. 57 Rhodehamel, 205.

p. 59 Norton, 203.

p. 59 Rhodehamel, 227.

p. 59 Crary, 166.

p. 60 Ibid., 61.

p. 61 Ibid.

p. 61 Rhodehamel, 242.

p. 63 Raphael, 63.

p. 63 Ibid., 64.

p. 63 Ibid.

p. 63 Ibid., 65.

p. 64 Rhodehamel, 523.

p. 64 Ibid., 524.

p. 64 Morris, 353.

p. 64 Raphael, 287.

p. 66 Ibid., 87.

p. 66 Ibid., 90.

p. 66 Rhodehamel, 372.

p. 66 Ibid.

p. 66 Albigence Waldo, quoted in Rhodehamel, 401.

p. 66–67 Ibid., 404.

p. 67 Ibid.

p. 67 Raphael, 86.

p. 67 Ibid.

p. 67 Ibid., 71.

p. 68 Israel Angell, quoted in Raphael, 88.

p. 69 Ibid., 311.

p. 69 Ibid.

p. 70 Ibid.

p. 70 Ibid.

p. 70 Rhodehamel, 654–655.

p. 71 Raphael, 121.

p. 71 Rhodehamel, 238.

p. 72 Raphael, 140.

p. 72 Buel and Buel, 105.

p. 72 Ibid., 106.

p. 73 Raphael, 114.

p. 73 Ibid.

p. 74 Norton, 220.

p. 74 Ibid., 216.

p. 74 Ibid., 200.

p. 75 Albert Cook Myers, ed., *Sally Wister's Journal: A True Narrative, 1777–1778* (Philadelphia: Ferris and Leach, 1902), 190.

p. 75 Raphael, 135.

p. 75 Norton, 199.

p. 75 Raphael, 136.

p. 75 Ibid.

p. 76 Ibid., 142.

p. 76 Ibid., 140.

p. 76 Ibid., 247.

p. 76 Ibid., 265.

p. 76 Ibid., 257.

p. 77 Rhodehamel, 304.

p. 78 Raphael, 196.

p. 79 Ibid., 221.

p. 79 Ibid., 224.

p. 79 Rhodehamel, 165.

p. 80 Raphael, 203.

p. 81 Rhodehamel, 415.

p. 81 Crary, 294.

p. 82 Ibid., 312.

p. 83 Morris, 273.

p. 83 Ibid.

p. 83 Ibid.

p. 83 Rhodehamel, 451.

p. 83 Crary, 318.

p. 84 McCullough, 16.

p. 85 Rhodehamel, 500.

p. 85 Raphael, 266.

p. 85 Ibid., 267.

p. 86 Ibid., 82.

p. 86 Ibid., 84.

p. 87 James Collins, quoted in Raphael, 158.

p. 87 Ibid., 4.

p. 87 Rhodehamel, 654.

p. 88 Raphael, 80.

p. 89 Ibid., 95.

p.89 Ibid., 119.

p. 89 Ibid., 91.

p. 89 Rhodehamel, 647.

p. 89 Ibid., 663.

p. 89 Ibid.

p. 90 Ebenezer Denny, *Military Journal of Major Ebenezer Denny* (Philadelphia: J. B. Lipincott, 1859), 34.

p. 91 Raphael, 296.

p. 91 Rhodehamel, 689.

p. 91 Ibid.

p. 91 Rhodehamel, 740.

p. 91 Crary, 346.

p. 92–93 Ibid., 354.

p. 93 Milton Meltzer, ed., *The American Revolutionaries: A History in Their Own Words, 1750–1800* (New York: Thomas Y. Crowell, 1987), 179.

p. 93 Crary, 367.

p. 93 Ibid.

p. 93 Rhodehamel, 790.

p. 93 Crary, 411–412.

p. 94 Jacqueline Jones, *American Work: Four Centuries of Black and White Labor* (New York: W. W. Norton, 1998), 143.

p. 94 Raphael, 290.

p. 95 Kanonraron, quoted in Raphael, 206.

p. 96 Crary, 410.

p. 96 Raphael, 102.

p. 97 Rhodehamel, 776.

p. 97 Ibid., 784.

p. 97 Ibid., 782.

p. 99 Ibid., 796.

p. 100 James Thomas Flexner, *Washington: The Indispensable Man* (1969; reprint, Boston: Little, Brown, 1974), 167.

SELECTED BIBLIOGRAPHY

Aptheker, Herbert. *A Documentary History of the Negro People in the United States.* Vol. 1. New York: Citadel, 1951.

Berlin, Ira, and Ronald Hoffman, eds. *Slavery and Freedom in the Age of the American Revolution.* Urbana: University of Illinois Press, 1986.

Buel, Joy Day, and Richard Bruel Jr. *The Way of Duty: A Woman and Her Family in Revolutionary America.* New York: W. W. Norton. 1984.

Crary, Catherine, ed. *The Price of Loyalty: Tory Writings from the Revolutionary Era.* New York: McGraw-Hill, 1973.

Denny, Ebenezer. *Military Journal of Major Ebenezer Denny.* Philadelphia: J. B. Lipincott, 1859.

Dudley, William, ed. *The American Revolution, Opposing Views.* San Diego: Greenhaven Press, 1992.

Gross, Robert. *The Minutemen and Their World.* New York: Hill and Wang, 1976.

McCullough, David. *John Adams.* New York: Simon and Schuster, 2001.

Morris, Richard, ed. *The American Revolution, 1763–1783: A Bicentennial Collection of Documents.* Columbia: University of South Carolina Press, 1970.

Myers, Albert Cook, ed. *Sally Wister's Journal: A True Narrative, 1777–1778.* Philadelphia: Ferris and Leach, 1902.

Norton, Mary Beth. *Liberty's Daughters: The Revolutionary Experience of American Women, 1750–1800.* New York: HarperCollins, 1980.

Raphael, Ray. *A People's History of the American Revolution: How Common People Shaped the Fight for Independence.* New York: The New Press, 2001.

Rhodehamel, John, comp. *The American Revolution, Writings from the War of Independence.* New York: The Library of America, 2001.

Smith, Carter, ed. *A Source Book on Colonial America: The Revolutionary War.* Brookfield, CT: Millbrook Press and The Library of Congress, 1991.

Wilbur, C. Keith, M.D. *Revolutionary Medicine, 1700–1800.* Old Saybrook, CT: The Globe Pequot Press, 1980.

FURTHER READING AND WEBSITES

Bober, Natalie. *Abigail Adams, Witness to a Revolution.* New York: Atheneum, 1995. This biography of First Lady Abigail Adams is a Boston Globe-Horn Book Award winner and provides a woman's perspective of the Revolution and the period.

Bohannon, Lisa Fredericksen. *The American Revolution.* Minneapolis: Lerner Publications Company, 2004. Learn more about the people, issues, and battles of the Revolutionary War.

Collier, James Lincoln, and Christopher Collier. *My Brother Sam Is Dead.* 1974. Reprint, New York: Scholastic, 1989. Through the eyes of the Meeker family, this historical novel and Newbery Honor book examines the issues and perspectives of the Revolutionary War that divided families and friendships.

Forbes, Esther. *Johnny Tremain.* 1944. Reprint, New York: Yearling, 1987. This historical novel and Newbery-Medal winner follows the life of a young silversmith caught up in the Revolutionary War.

Freedman, Russell. *Give Me Liberty: The Story of the Declaration of Independence.* New York: Holiday House, 2000. Descriptive text and excerpts from primary source materials tell the story of the Declaration of Independence and the American Revolution.

Marrin, Albert. *George Washington and the Founding of a Nation.* New York: Dutton, 2001. Find balanced information on the Revolution in this biography of General and President George Washington.

Meltzer, Milton. *The American Revolutionaries: A History in Their Own Words, 1750–1800*. New York: Thomas Y. Crowell, 1987. Learn more about the Revolution through excerpts of letters, journals, reports, and official documents of the period.

Miller, Brandon Marie. *Growing Up in Revolution and the New Nation*. Minneapolis: Lerner Publications Company, 2004. This book examines the lives of young people during the Revolution.

The American Revolution: Maps and Charts, 1750–1789. http://memory. loc.gov/ammem/gmdhtml/armhtml/armhome.html. Researchers will find a searchable database of Revolutionary War era maps.

An American Time Capsule: Three Centuries of Broadsides and Other Printed Ephemera. http://memory.loc.gov/ammem/rbpehtml/pehome. html. This Library of Congress site offers a searchable database of proclamations, printed notices, advertisements, and other printed matter, including the colonial period and the Revolution.

Complete Research Resource: Boston Massacre. http://www.bostonmassacre. net/index.html. This site from the Boston Historical Society provides researchers with a rich history of the Boston Massacre through text, images, and period documents.

George Washington Papers at the Library of Congress http://memory.loc. gov/ammem/gwhtml/gwhome.html. Read the personal and official writings of General and President George Washington.

The Thomas Jefferson Papers. http://memory.loc.gov/ammem/mtjhtml/ mtjhome.html. Access the historical writings of this Patriot and early president, including draft fragments of the Declaration of Independence and war correspondence.

U.S. Congressional Documents and Debates, 1774–1873. http://memory. loc.gov/ammem/amlaw/lawhome.html. Through this site, students can access early congressional journals and debates, as well as letters of the delegates to the First and Second Continental Congresses.

INDEX

ACKNOWLEDGMENTS

The images in this book are used with the permission of: National Archives, pp. 2, 24 [W&C 3], 37 [W&C 11], 40 [W&C 15], 46 [W&C 18], 51 [W&C 19], 53 [W&C 20], 57 [W&C 28], 61 [NWDNS-111-SC-83397], 62 [W&C 70], 78 [Rev War 46], 80 [W&C 33], 84 [W&C 26], 98 [W&C 55]; courtesy of the Library of Congress, pp. 6 [LC-USZ62-242], 7 [LC-USZ62-7819], 11 [LC-USZ62-45564], 13 [LC-USZ62-3775], 17 [LC-USZ62-1505], 20 [LC-USZC4-4600], 22 [LC-USZ62-12711], 25 [Rare Book and Special Collections Division, Portfolio 347, Folder 10], 26 [LC-USZ62-11139], 28 [LC-USZ62-45328], 30 [LC-USZ62-45556], 33 [LC-USZ62-45586], 34 [LC-DIG-ppmsca-05483], 38 [LC-USZ62-21488], 44 [LC-USZ62-45198], 48 [LC-USZ62-45532], 50 [LC-USZ62-45549], 55 [Rare Book and Special Collections Division, Continental Congress & Constitutional Convention Broadsides Collection no. 8], 58 [LC-USZC4-1262], 65 [LC-USZ62-704], 74 [LC-USZ62-8452], 75 [LC-USZ62-44892], 81 [LC-USZ62-62548], 82 [Manuscript Division, George Washington Papers], 85 [Manuscript Division, Thomas Jefferson Papers], 87 [LC-USZC4-5280], 88 [LC-USZ6-864], 92 [Manuscript Division, George Washington Papers], 94 [LC-USZC4-5321], 96 [LC-USZ62-45500], 97 [Law Library, Journals of the Continental Congress, Volume 24], 103 [Manuscript Division, Thomas Jefferson Papers]; Laura Westlund, p. 8; © North Wind Picture Archives, pp. 12, 72, 90; Getty Images, pp. 14, 18, 77, 86; © Bettmann/CORBIS, pp. 23, 60, 68; Independent Picture Service (IPS), pp. 33 (inset), 47; © Freelance Photography Guild/CORBIS, p. 35.

Cover: William Walcutt, "Pulling Down the Statue of George III at Bowling Green" (detail) /Kirby Collection of Historical Paintings, Lafayette College Art Collection, Easton, Pennsylvania.

Back cover and flaps: National Archive.

TITLES FROM THE AWARD-WINNING PEOPLE'S HISTORY SERIES:

For more information, please visit www.lernerbooks.com